ELEMENTARY P.E. TEACHER'S SURVIVAL GUIDE

Here's everything
you need to create a successful
student-centered physical education program,
complete with reproducible forms,
activity sheets, exercise worksheets,
award certificates, and more!

Jeff Carpenter & Diane Tunnell

PARKER PUBLISHING COMPANY
West Nyack, New York 10995

Library of Congress Cataloging-in-Publication Data

Carpenter, Jeff.
    Elementary P.E. teacher's survival guide / Jeff Carpenter & Diane
Tunnell.
       p.   cm.
    ISBN 0-13-302993-X
    1. Physical education for children.   2. Physical education for
children—Study and teaching (Activity programs)   I. Tunnell,
Diane.   II. Title.   III. Title: Elementary physical education
teacher's survival guide.
    GV443.C37   1994   94-2806
    372.86—dc20   CIP

Printed in the United States of America

10 9 8 7 6 5 4 3

ISBN 0-13-302993-X

 PARKER PUBLISHING COMPANY
West Nyack, NY 10994

A Simon & Schuster Company

On the World Wide Web at http://www.phdirect.com

Prentice-Hall International (UK) Limited, *London*
Prentice-Hall of Australia Pty. Limited, *Sydney*
Prentice-Hall Canada Inc., *Toronto*
Prentice-Hall Hispanoamericana, S.A., *Mexico*
Prentice-Hall of India Private Limited, *New Delhi*
Prentice-Hall of Japan, Inc., *Tokyo*
Simon & Schuster Asia Pte. Ltd., *Singapore*
Editora Prentice-Hall do Brasil, Ltda., *Rio de Janeiro*

Dedicated to
Jonathan and Brad.
May you both develop
the skills and knowledge necessary
to grow and lead healthy and active lifestyles.

ACKNOWLEDGMENTS

The authors gratefully acknowledge the assistance provided by the following professionals for their efforts in compiling this guide: Alice-Elizabeth Carpenter, M.A., Olympia Public Schools; Kelly Rankin, Ed.D., Vancouver Public Schools; Al Tweit, Olympia Public Schools; TNT Design Studios, Olympia, illustrators; and Barbara Diment, typist.

Foreword

The *Elementary P.E. Teacher's Survival Guide* represents a positive step in bringing together student-centered activities in a format that is understandable to classroom teachers and physical educators alike. Jeff Carpenter and Diane Tunnell have brought together their combined talents and expertise, developed over years of practical teaching experience and research, to provide a guide that presents developmentally appropriate activities that have been shown to be appealing and motivational to children. The activities presented will assist teachers in preparing lessons that provide for student success each day in both the gym and classroom.

Having had the opportunity to work directly with Jeff and Diane, I know their dedication to the enhancement of each student's life through the development of a healthy lifestyle has been clearly articulated in this guide. It will be not only useful but also motivational to both teachers and students.

KELLY R. RANKIN, ED.D.
Physical Education
    Curriculum Specialist
Vancouver School District
Vancouver, Washington

About the Authors

Jeff Carpenter, M.S.P.E., taught elementary, middle, and high school physical education for 15 years before becoming Washington State Supervisor of Physical Education in 1985. Jeff's active presentations at national, state, and regional conferences—including the National AAHPERD Convention and the President's Council on Physical Fitness & Sports Regional Workshops—continually receive excellent reviews. His professional involvement includes terms as President of the Washington Alliance for HPERD and service on numerous regional and national committees. The author of two other books and numerous articles, Jeff has received many awards and citations by the state of Washington, including Physical Educator of the Year and the Meritorious Service Award.

Diane Tunnell, Ed. D., has taught innovative methods classes at the university level and K–12 physical education for the past 18 years. Her numerous articles and presentations on instructional methods and interdisciplinary approaches to enhancing student knowledge have continually received superb recognition. Diane's ability to develop innovative activities designed for student success creates a caring environment in which all students are active learners. She is currently an Associate Professor of Physical Education and the Department Chairperson at Gonzaga University in Spokane, Washington.

About This Guide

The *Elementary P.E. Teacher's Survival Guide* is designed to be used as a foundation for program development and implementation to enhance student fitness levels. As demonstrated by these activities, all students must be given varied experiences based on individual considerations and presented in a variety of instructional settings that provide for successful acquisition of lifelong activity patterns.

The book is centered on the developmental concept of providing activities based on the characteristics of students according to their age, maturation level, and physical capabilities. A developmental program should be progressive in nature, building upon previous experiences and activities. It is necessary for you to note the *individual* developmental level of your students as well as the total group. In traditional physical education classes one would see lines of students all performing several exercises in unison. While there is a time and place for this type of structure, placing an emphasis on more individual, student-centered, success-oriented, creative, and motivational activities that will accomplish the same goals is something physical educators and classroom teachers should be striving toward.

This guide provides you with over 100 activities that will allow for the development of motor skills, physical fitness, and many sports skills. Care must be taken to ensure that proper exercise techniques by taught and applied by all students in order to achieve maximum benefit and reduce the potential risk of injury. These activities are not unique by themselves, but when mixed together with other innovative components, they develop not only fitness but also motor skills. To be able to combine these and to provide motivation for the students to participate will help move us toward the goal of a program where all students are actively engaged in meaningful work and experience success each day.

Each activity presented has been successfully used by elementary and middle-level physical educators and classroom teachers alike in a variety of school settings. From large urban/suburban schools to small rural locations, these activities and instructional formats have provided for student success. The activities are presented in an easy-to-follow format. Each activity includes a listing of the focus area along with a brief description that contains an overview of the total activity. This is followed by a step-by-step listing of the procedure and any necessary diagrams of facility set-up and student movement patterns. In addition, organizational, safety, and modification hints are provided to make the teaching process easier and spark your imagination.

Section 1, "Getting Started Toward Student Success," provides guidelines for the successful development and implementation of a student-centered physical education program designed for maximum participation and student success. You'll find specific information regarding program outcomes, facility management, fitness testing, student safety, class organization and management, scheduling, specific responsibilities of school staff, and a sound basis on which to begin formulating your programs utilizing activities found in later sections.

Section 2, "Fitness Activities," provides 46 activities for the fitness component of the instructional program. You'll find the basic exercises—as well as some not often used—for providing a creative way to enhance student participation.

Section 3, "Skill Challenges and Motivators," combines fitness with skill development. The 44 activities provide ideas ranging from traditional activities, such as volleyball and basketball, to alternative activities with unique equipment.

Section 4, "Interdisciplinary Activities for Fitness," is designed to be incorporated throughout the year. It provides a conceptual base for including fitness and activities into the daily lives of all students. This section is an ideal way to connect theory lessons with practical application situations, strengthening the joining of the classroom and the gymnasium. The classroom teacher can introduce the concepts in a lesson related to health, for example, and the physical education specialist can use a variety of the activities to reinforce the concept. These 11 activities also provide an excellent base for homework assignments that can involve both parents and students.

Section 5, "Communications and Special Programs," presents basic information regarding the promotion of quality physical education programs using newsletters, oral presentations, the media, and various student demonstrations. Each of the activities listed has been proven to be successful in a variety of situations in local school districts. In addition, this section provides information on the planning and organization of student-centered Play Days, and how students can be involved with the design and implementation of these activities.

It is our hope that the activities and concepts presented in *Elementary P.E. Teacher's Survival Guide* will not only be useful, but will also spark your imagination to create additional activities and routines to benefit all students.

JEFF CARPENTER
DIANE TUNNELL

Instructional Considerations for Including Developmental Fitness Activities for Your Program

Class Procedures

As students enter the physical education facility, they are psychologically prepared for activity. Therefore, you should take full advantage of this enthusiasm and prepare them for more vigorous activity.

Depending upon the structure of the program, once students are prepared to participate, they should be instructed to immediately begin a stretching program lasting for approximately five minutes. With younger students, be prepared to lead these activities for the first part of the year. With older students, once procedures and routines are established, the program cn be posted so students can begin on their own. At the conclusion of the stretching phase, give directions to move into the next activity—the developmental fitness portion.

Safety

Care must be taken in conducting any strenous exercise program. It is your responsibility to determine if any student has a physically limiting condition that may preclude him or her participating in the activities, to ensure a safe facility, and to make certain all presented exercises are performed in a safe and appropriate manner.

Over the years scientific research has had a tremendous impetus regarding the advancement of physical activities and performance. We are more aware today of the effects of improper training and incorrect exercise techniques. Therefore, when conducting exercises, be aware of the literature reviews that have lead to modification in performing certain exercises.

Stretching activities requiring bending forward, such as Leg Stretches or the Sit and Reach, should be performed with the knee joint slightly relaxed rather than in a locked position. This will help avoid hyperextension of the knee joint. Perform all stretches using a static, rather than ballistic motion, holding the position for a minimum of 20 seconds. Avoid activities that flex a joint past a 90-degree angle such as the traditional "hurdler stretch."

When performing abdominal exercises, including Curl-Ups and related activities, students should have their knees bent, feet flat on the floor, and arms folded over the chest. If the students cannot perform the Curl-Up without assistance or in the suggested position, there are several modifications; for example, put hands on the thighs and curl up until the palms have crossed the knee before returning to the floor, or have a partner hold the feet. During these types of exercises, the chin should be tucked and the individual should only curl to approximately 45 degrees. Aerobic activities are designed to increase an individual's heart rate and develop a greater efficiency of the cardiovascular system. Some general guidelines and precautions should be considered when introducing students to the cardiovascular component of the program:

- Start slow and work in small increments to the maximum time noted
- do not expect all students to begin at the same level
- when jogging, students should not be "out of breath"; if a student complains of

chest pains or breathing difficulties, have him or her stop immediately and seek assistance

Some basic guidelines to follow when exercising include: don't lock or hyperextend a joint; don't bounce when stretching; don't arch the lower back or neck; don't swing; and don't overflex a joint. By being aware of some simple guidelines, the exercise program will be safe, productive, and have positive results for all students.

Resources

Bennett, John P., and Artie Kamiya. *Fun and Fitness for Everyone*. Durham, NC: Great Activities, 1986.

Melson, Bob, and Vicki Worrell. *Rope Skipping for Fun and Fitness*. Wichita, KS: Woodlawn Publisher, Inc., 1986.

Pangrazi, Robert P., and Victor P. Dauer. *Dynamic Physical Education of Elementary School Children*. New York: Macmillan, 1992.

Poppen, Jerry. *Action Packet on Jump Rope: Individual Rope Skills*. Puyallup, WA: Action Productions, 1989.

Seagraves, Margaret C. *Move to Learn*. Winston-Salem, NC: Hunter, 1979.

Short, Kathryn. *Physical Education Is More Than Just Kickball*. Brea, CA: Kathryn Short Productions, 1990.

Turner, Lowell, and Susan Turner. *PE Teacher's Skill-by-Skill Activities Program*. West Nyack, NY: Parker Publishing Company, 1989.

Contents

Section 1
GETTING STARTED TOWARD STUDENT SUCCESS • 1

Section 2
FITNESS ACTIVITIES • 25

Section 3
SKILL CHALLENGES AND MOTIVATORS • 139

Softball Skills and Fitness

Volleyball Skills and Fitness

Section 4
INTERDISCIPLINARY ACTIVITIES FOR FITNESS • 273

Section 5
COMMUNICATIONS AND SPECIAL PROGRAMS • 325

1

Getting Started Toward Student Success

Getting Started Toward Student Success

A PROGRAM OVERVIEW

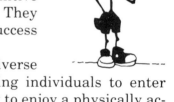

What Is Physical Education?

Today's physical education programs maintain the traditional objectives in the areas of physical development (fitness and skills) and neuromuscular development (efficient movement), cognitive development, and affective development (social-emotional). They also offer much more in providing for student-centered and success oriented activities to enhance the traditional objectives.

Planned purposeful physical education will provide a diverse program of student-centered instructional activities allowing individuals to enter adult life with the skills, knowledge, and attitudes necessary to enjoy a physically active and healthy lifestyle.

Why Is Physical Education Essential?

Educators, parents, and students are now realizing the potential for learning that is inherent in a well-planned and coordinated physical education program. Today's student-centered and success-oriented programs maintain traditional objectives in the physiological development (fitness and skills) and neurological development (nervous system) of all students. A planned purposeful physical education today will offer much more. It provides:

- a wide range of knowledge and movement experiences so each student may develop competencies that are both adaptable and versatile

- an opportunity to experience a sense of achievement and develop a positive self-image and self-concept

- an opportunity to experience the learning process of inquiry and exploration

- a learning atmosphere providing opportunities for all students to analyze, think, observe, discuss, create, cooperate, and share

- experiences and information for all students to develop a positive, active, and healthy lifestyle

New Directions Changing educational and cultural forces have given a "new look" and new directions to physical education programs. There has also been a tremendous surge of interest in developing new delivery systems to motivate *all* students

regardless of race, sex, size, or previous experience. Gone are the days when physical education was largely a recreational period composed of games and sports, the purpose of which was mostly to provide a change of pace in the school day and prepare for extracurricular activities.

Perhaps the greatest change in the field can be attributed to an emerging educational climate. The following statements from Kelly Rankin's *PE Guidelines for School Administrators* (Olympia, WA: OSPI, 1989) represent a new focus and important changes to keep in mind when developing quality programs for students:

- From a program that stresses activities to one that calls attention to the student as an individual.
- From learning that takes place only in the classroom to one that takes place in the entire school, including the gymnasium.
- From institutional content (what the school thinks is important) to learner content (what the learner thinks is important).
- From an educational offering accountable to itself to one that is accountable to the consumer—students, parents, and community.
- From a program that is an end in itself to one that focuses on physical education as a means to an end—the total development of a child.
- From teaching geared to one learning style to utilization of varied teaching-learning styles.
- From a program that establishes a uniform pace for all children to one that centers on the individual and his or her rate of progress.
- From just a "what" curriculum to a "what, why, and how" curriculum.
- From sporadic emphasis on ego development to a systematic approach for the development of self-concept and cultural identity.
- From standards that are arbitrary to ones that focus on success by assuring a learning environment in which each student can succeed.
- From one that is taught in isolation to one that relates to other learning areas of the curriculum.

Student-Centered Outcomes Each curricular area within a school should make a strong contribution to the educational process. Physical education serves to complement other educational areas, in addition to promoting educational outcomes that are not likely to be achieved in other subject areas. The physical education contributions are expressed through the following student-centered outcomes:

Participate actively in physical activity and attain appropriate levels of physical fitness.

Through a sufficiently challenging program, a child should be afforded the opportunity to develop personal levels of strength, endurance, flexibility, and body composition commensurate with his or her needs and interests.

Develop movement competency.

This goal infers an instructional program allowing each child to develop reasonable competencies in movement so he or she may move with personal satisfaction and participate actively with his or her peers. The degree of success the child experiences in work and play is influenced by his or her ability to execute movement patterns effectively and efficiently.

Foster creativity.

Each child should be provided an opportunity to express understanding of self and his or her environment through movement.

Emphasize safety practices.

Morally and legally a teacher simply cannot turn children loose and hope for the best. Each child needs to consider the responsibilities to self and to his or her peers with respect to conducting movement patterns in a safe manner. It is the clear responsibility of all school personnel to see that this is accomplished.

Motivate expression and communication.

Movement is one of the most often used means the child employs in nonverbal communication and expression. The child needs access to a wide variety of physical education tools, including manipulative equipment, small and large apparatus, games, and sports activities.

Promote self-understanding and acceptance.

Students need to work at their own level, achieve success, and avoid extended periods of frustration. Students who are successful will progress and gain satisfaction from their experiences.

To accomplish these outcomes the instructional program must provide activities that can serve as vehicles for successful accomplishment, and the learning experiences involved must be guided and directed so the attainment of the outcomes is assured. If the outcomes are to be accomplished, the physical education program will be largely an instructional program, with the recreational aspects growing out of planned learning experiences taught in progressive sequences.

PROGRAM GUIDELINES FOR STUDENT SUCCESS AND MOTIVATION

In each class teachers find themselves dealing with students having varied backgrounds, experiences, and proficiencies. The following guidelines should be considered in the development and implementation of a stimulating learning environment designed to have *all* students actively engaged and experiencing success each day.

- The program should have, as its basis, a common core of body management competencies serving as a foundation for basic and specialized skills.
- The program should serve all students—regardless of ability.

- It should be geared to the development and educational needs of each child.
- The program should stimulate each child to maximum involvement in activities, calling for mental, motor, and emotional responses, leading to desirable modification in behavior skills, knowledge, and attitudes.
- Special attention is needed for those children who exhibit movement problems and/or are physically underdeveloped.
- There should be a variety of movement experiences, games, sports, gymnastic-type activities, rhythms and dance, fitness activities, alternative activities, and—when available—aquatics.
- The activities of the program should feature sequential arrangement of learning experiences, emphasizing progression in and between grade levels.
- The instructional program should encourage vigorous physical activity and lead to the attainment of desirable levels of fitness.
- Individual learning should be predominant and consideration for individual differences should be made. Provision, however, should also be made for group experiences.
- The choice of both learning experiences and approaches should be based on the characteristics, needs, maturity level, and prior experiences of the children.
- Sufficient supplies and equipment should be present so individualized learning can take place with little waiting for turns or the sharing of equipment and supplies.
- Where possible and feasible, the physical education program should supplement and integrate with other educational experiences.

ACTIVITY AREAS

Each day students need a planned program of physical activity that includes five basic component areas: Readiness Activities; Core Fitness Development; Skill-Building Instruction/Practice; Games and Sports; and Gymnastics. While the bulk of this guide focuses on activities designed to develop physical fitness through a variety of activities, the following provides a brief overview of the five component areas.

Readiness Activities

Research and practice tells us when students come to physical education classes, they are prepared to be active. In order to meet this need and establish a "tone" for activity and success, we must provide a quick, low-organized movement activity. This activity should last for approximately three minutes during which time roll may be taken or equipment set up.

Sample Activities
1. Ask for random locomotor activities around the facility. Have students jump, leap, or hop over each line.
2. Have jump ropes placed around the perimeter of the facility. Each student picks up a rope upon entering and begins to jump.
3. Set up challenge stations around the facility; for example, jump rope, juggling, basketball hoop shot, pogo sticks, rocketballs, chin-ups, etc. Have students go to a station and perform the activity for three minutes. At the end of the time limit, have students record their achievement on a card. File the card until their next attempt and see if they can improve their score.

Core Fitness Activities

The attainment of suitable levels of physical fitness is an objective unique to physical education. To be strong and able to meet physical challenges is a desire for all children. The physical education program should offer activities of sufficient intensity to develop the various qualities (strength, endurance, flexibility, and body composition) of fitness. It should be structured so all major muscle groups are exercised, paying particular attention to the cardiorespiratory system, the arm-shoulder region, and abdominal region.

A more formalized fitness program begins to be implemented beginning in the third grade. During this time the various routines and activities discussed in Section 2 of this guide would be presented. These activities include various forms of circuit training, games, teacher/leader routines, and cooperative activities chosen for their developmental potential.

A key to fitness development is to provide activities that will allow for a physical challenge and muscular work in a time frame sufficient to meet the developmental needs of the students. Another key is variety. Long periods of formal regimented exercises can and often do turn children away from an active fitness-oriented lifestyle now and in the future. The ideas and activities presented in Section 2 provide 8 to 15 minutes of activity and a schedule of activity variation designed to meet the needs and abilities of all students.

Skill-Building Instruction/Practice Activities

When determining the daily lesson you should provide approximately 20 minutes or 50 percent of the available time to this component. In addition to actual instruction, students must be given sufficient time for directed practice. In keeping with the concept of all students actively engaged and successful each day, planning must revolve around total student involvement. Section 3 provides student-centered activities in various skill-building components leading towards fitness and skill development while providing for student success. Included in skill-building instruction are movement activities, rhythmic activities, games and sports, and gymnastic activities. Movement experiences include activities known as "Basic Movement," which stress movement based on the concepts of force, time, space, and flow. Specifically, this area should include movement from one place to another (locomotor movement), movements done in place (nonlocomotor movements), and manipulative activities with balls, beanbags, hoops, wands, etc. Also included are experiences on a variety of large apparatus such as boxes, beams, benches, climbing ropes, wall-attached climbing frames, portable floor-climbing apparatus, mats, etc.

Rhythmic activities embrace fundamental rhythms, creative rhythms, manipulative apparatus to rhythm, singing games, folk dances, square dances, and other nontraditional dance forms.

Games and Sports

This area should include the simple, low-organized games, relays, and the individual/dual/team sport skills appropriate to individual student skill levels as well as grade level.

Gymnastic Activities

These activities include tumbling, stunts, activities on apparatus, and the area generally defined as self-testing or alternative activities (unicycle, pogo sticks, juggling, etc.).

GAMES

At the close of each lesson students at all levels have the need to participate in a low-organized fun activity. This activity should be designed to provide each student with a feeling of success and enjoyment from the day's experiences. Included in this 3- to 5-minute period should be relays, noncompetitive games, cooperation activities, etc.

TESTING IN PHYSICAL FITNESS

Testing in the area of physical fitness has several educationally sound purposes. First, it can measure whether or not the developmental needs of the students have been met. Second, it can identify physically underdeveloped students who merit special attention. A third value lies in the motivation provided by a testing program. Finally, the use of fitness-testing results provides definite evidence of the value of this component of the physical education program. **However, care**

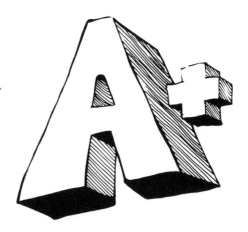

must be exercised not to judge the value of the entire program solely on fitness scores.

Testing should be done a minimum of twice a year—at the beginning and end of the school year or, as many successful programs have experienced, year-round testing with multiple trials.

The multiple-trial format allows a student to take a test component several times throughout the year with the best attempt being recorded as the "final" score. This format allows students to continually focus on improving fitness levels and provide them with continued feedback, thus eliminating the idea of fitness being only a "two-time-per-year component."

Sample Multiple-Trial Format

October:	Complete fitness test given to all students.
	Teacher meets with students to discuss results and provide assistance in development of personal improvement plan.
November:	Every Wednesday 10 minutes of the period is given to review fitness testing. Student records scores and reviews with teacher.
December:	Continue one-day-per-week testing program.
January:	Complete fitness test given to all students.
	Teacher meets with students to discuss results and provide assistance in development of personal fitness improvement plan.
February–April:	Continue one-day-per-week testing program.
May:	Complete fitness test given to all students.
	Teacher meets with students to discuss results and provide assistance in the development of a summer plan for fitness improvement.

PROGRAM FOR THE PHYSICALLY UNDERFIT STUDENT

After a child has been identified as being in the lowest quartile as determined by a standardized fitness test, the next step is to set up a program to improve individual achievement. Several items are important to consider in this process.

First, it must be determined no personal health conditions are present that may contribute to or cause the underdeveloped status. This may involve an examination by a physician. The second item of consideration relates to health habits of the child (nutrition, rest, home conditions, etc.) which may shed light on the problem. Corrective action for these two items should proceed as indicated and approved by school policy and regulation.

Once the student's physical condition and health habits have been considered, the next step is to prescribe a program of physical activity the student should participate in to raise his or her fitness/skill levels. This action can take place in special sessions with the physical education staff, special classes, specified homework assignments, or concentrated efforts such as summer fitness/skill sessions.

Sample Program for Students with Low Fitness Levels

Children selected for this program would be those whose demonstrated levels of physical fitness are well below the developmentally appropriate levels as determined by a valid assessment instrument. It is estimated this would include only 10–20 students in any school.

After being selected, a conference is held with each student to secure a commitment that he or she will participate in the program and will take responsibility for raising his or her level of fitness to an appropriate level. At this time it is also important to communicate with the parents to explain the program, determine that no medical problems are the basis for the low levels of fitness (parents should be encouraged to have a physician examine the child and make recommendations prior to beginning the program), and to secure their commitment to assisting the child in meeting established goals. Parents must also understand the need to support their child through encouragement and understanding rather than forcing the child to participate. It is essential the child, not the teacher or parent, accept the responsibility for improvement. By acceptance of responsibility the child will gain a positive self-image through his or her accomplishments as well as be more likely to achieve agreed-upon goals.

Implementation   Each student is given a "contract" providing an overview of the program and general statements regarding "What Is Physical Fitness," "How Can Being Physically Fit Help You Lead a Healthier and More Productive Life," and "How Can You Take Responsibility for Your Activity and Fitness Levels." After the student understands the program, he or she is provided with an "Activity Journal and Goal Folder." (See the sample contract.)

It is important for you to go over each activity with the student to insure each activity is understood and is within the ability of the student. At the weekly meeting with the student, you should "spot check" progress and modify activities accordingly. In addition, a weekly note should go to the parent indicating what progress has been made and promoting continued support.

(Sample Contract)*

ACTIVITY JOURNAL AND GOALS FOR:

(Student's name)

To improve your levels of physical fitness it is important that you participate in your selected exercise program along with active leisure-time pursuits. The following selected activities should be completed daily. At the weekly meeting with your teacher, this plan will be reviewed and modified to continue meeting your needs. Good luck!

1. **IMPROVING FLEXIBILITY:** Do each of the following daily.

Sit and Reach	3 repetitions, holding for 30 seconds each
Side Flex	4 repetitions each side, holding for 20 seconds each
V-Sit and Reach	3 repetitions, holding for 30 seconds each

2. **IMPROVING UPPER-BODY STRENGTH:** Choose three of the following to do daily.

Modified Pull-Ups	1 daily
	or
Flexed Arm Hang	25 seconds each day
Your Push-Up Modification	10 each day
Crab Walk	Go 15 feet, walk back to the start line; repeat 5 times
Selected Isometrics	Hold each for 15 seconds, do 3 repetitions of each

3. **IMPROVING ABDOMINAL STRENGTH:** Do each of the following daily.

Partial Curl-Up	15—2 sets
Lower Down	15—2 sets
Leg Pushes	15—2 sets

4. **IMPROVING CARDIOVASCULAR ENDURANCE:** Do one activity daily.

Brisk Walking	20 minutes
Jogging/Walking	20 minutes
Rope Skipping	15 minutes

5. **GENERAL ACTIVITIES:** Do one or more of the following 2 to 3 times per week.

Bicycling	Skiing	Roller Skating
Soccer	Hiking	Swimming
Basketball	Baseball	Racquet Sports

*The activities listed are only examples. Actual activities will vary depending on the abilities and interests of individual students.

STUDENT NEEDS AND CHARACTERISTICS

Grades K-2

The primary child, who usually has a "me" attitude, is individualistic, creative, uninhibited, and often rhythmic. Although these skills lack preciseness, they are developing at a steady rate. Along with general skill development, hand-eye coordination is developing, allowing most second-grade students to handle objects effectively.

At this age, the child needs a wide variety of large muscle experiences involving both locomotor and nonlocomotor movements. Manipulative experiences with small apparatus—beanbags, balls, hoops, wands, etc.—contribute to hand-eye coordination and the acquisition of sports-related skills and physical fitness.

Grades 3-5

In this age group, coordination, reaction time, and strength are improved to the extent that children can absorb more complex skills and sequences. More time is spent on sports skills, but with stress on the development of skills more so than the competitive aspects. Games and other group activities provide for enhancement of cooperative skills.

Students in this age group have developed a greater attention span, allowing for longer and more concentrated periods of efforts. Children can work towards the goal of quality movement as they can intellectualize the instructional process in their quest of a skill. They are also able to develop an expanded attitude towards the importance of fitness and have a need to be provided with numerous opportunities to enhance their physical fitness and skill levels.

While the application of movement education principles and approaches are still important, the methodologies move towards drawing more specific responses.

Grades 6–8

The period of transition is often one of stresses, strains, and a sometimes "illogical" upheaval in the student's emotional, social, intellectual, and physical worlds. It is also a period of great physical change. Physical education programs should include a systematic curriculum of instruction in a wide variety of activities to provide a transition from the elementary program.

These activities should include skills and concepts in the areas of conditioning and fitness; individual, dual, and team sports; gymnastics; dance; aquatics; alternative activities; and recreational games. These experiences must be planned and implemented in a manner maximizing their contribution to the overall goals of education and providing the maximum benefit to each individual student.

IMPLEMENTING AN EFFECTIVE PHYSICAL EDUCATION PROGRAM

It is important the entire school community accept the fundamental premise that physical education is a developmental and instructional program which is an integral part of the total educational experience for each child. A team effort involving the school administration, principals, supervisors, teachers, and parents is needed to insure a quality program. The responsibilities of each of the groups are defined in turn.

Responsibilities of the School District

- Determines the direction of the physical education program to meet statutory regulations.
- Insures the total separation between the athletic programs and those of physical education.

- Takes the lead in establishing success-oriented programs for all students.
- Provides facilities, equipment, instructional supplies, and qualified personnel necessary to operate a quality program.
- Periodically reviews and evaluates the program based on student needs.
- Provides effective dissemination of program highlights to the public.
- Encourages the development of a district physical education curriculum based on research and "best practices."
- Establishes a district-wide physical education committee with broad representation from physical education personnel, regular teaching staff, administration, medical community, parents, students, and the general public.

Responsibilities of the Principal

- Periodically evaluates the physical education program with teachers, supervisors, and other interested individuals/groups.
- Maintains the separation of physical education and the athletic program in the areas of budget, supplies, equipment, and staff.
- Provides for effective scheduling of physical education instructional periods to assure maximum utilization of teaching stations.
- Maintains a safety program for activities with proper supervision and rules of conduct.
- Provides for continuous and periodic inspection of facilities and equipment.
- Establishes long-range plans for facility development and revolving equipment replacement.
- Assures appropriate standards of curriculum conformance and continuity, and educationally sound instructional approaches.
- Provides inservice education opportunities for all staff teaching physical education.

Responsibilities of the Physical Educator

- Functions as contributing and participating member of the school staff.
- Assists with the determination of needs and the planning of student-centered programs.
- Provides a high-quality program based on the district curriculum.
- On a regular basis, assists elementary classroom teachers who have responsibility of teaching their own physical education classes.
- Provides for evaluation of the program by requesting feedback from students, teachers, administrators, and parents.
- Is sensitive to the needs of and gives special help to students with special needs, slow learners, physically handicapped, and underdeveloped.
- Maintains high professional standards.
- Observes all safety standards while conducting activities.
- Maintains appropriate amounts of equipment and supplies through either repair or replacement. Provides positive input into selection and purchase.

- Provides appropriate curriculum and instruction to separate the athletic program and physical education.

Responsibilities of the Classroom Teacher

- Plans and carries out an instructional physical education program as prescribed by the district.
- Provides for quick and orderly movement of children between the classroom and the physical education teaching area.
- Participates in the evaluation of the physical education program.
- Allots sufficient time for planning physical education experiences so that the instruction is based on an effective lesson plan.
- Takes part in inservice training as scheduled.
- Asks for assistance when needed.
- Provides for orderly issue and return of required equipment and supplies.
- Dresses appropriately for the instruction, usually with at least a change of shoes.

Responsibilities of the Parents

- Sees that each child has the proper attire for physical education classes.
- Makes appropriate decisions with respect to asking for students to be excused from activity, recognizing that this should only be done for proper cause.
- Becomes sufficiently informed of the philosophy and objectives of the physical education program and demands that the school operate a program that is student-centered and oriented to individual success.
- Is willing and able to make suggestions for program modification or adjustments.

SCHEDULING A QUALITY PROGRAM

The scheduling of physical education classes is an administrative responsibility because all classes must use the same facility. A way must be found to give all classes an opportunity to use these facilities. The larger the school enrollment, the greater the problem of scheduling. If the characteristics of children at the elementary level and the objectives of physical education are understood, certain limitations or guiding principles concerning scheduling become apparent. These principles are:

- A daily period of physical education for every child is necessary.
- The physical education class should not be less than 30 minutes in length in grades K–5 and 50 minutes in grades 6–8.
- If children change clothes for physical education, an additional 8–10 minutes must be allowed.
- Two or more physical education classes should not be combined with one teacher for instruction.

In a small elementary school the scheduling of daily physical education classes is not usually a problem. The most suitable time under these conditions would be during the middle of the day. By blocking this time for physical education, the facility may be prepared and equipment left in place from one class to the next. It is also best to block the primary grades and the intermediate grades "back to back," thus minimizing equipment movement.

Scheduling is more difficult in larger schools, especially if a daily program is provided. Under these circumstances the combining of classes may be appropriate if student-teacher ratios are maintained, more than one teacher is present, and the facilities and equipment are appropriate for the number of students participating. Due to lack of staff and facility/equipment, this format is not always possible; therefore, the use of alternating days of physical education is more appropriate. When utilizing an alternate-day schedule, students must be given appropriate physical education homework (see Section 6) and the classroom teacher must provide instruction that integrates physical education concepts into the regular classroom instruction (see Section 5).

Sample Schedules

Small Elementary

10:00–10:30	grade 1
10:30–11:00	grade 2
11:00–11:30	grade 3
1:00–1:30	grade 4
1:30–2:00	grade 5

Large Elementary (single classes—alternating days):

DAY 1:

9:00–9:30	grade 1
9:30–10:00	grade 2
10:30–11:00	grade 3
11:00–11:30	grade 4
1:00–1:30	grade 5
1:30–2:00	grade 5
2:30–3:00	grade 5

DAY 2:

9:00–9:30	grade 1
9:30–10:00	grade 1
10:30–11:00	grade 2
11:00–11:30	grade 2
1:00–1:30	grade 3
1:30–2:00	grade 3
2:30–3:00	grade 4
3:00–3:30	grade 4

At grades 6–8, the middle level, students are usually scheduled through the "master schedule" for the school. The physical education staff and facility must be of appropriate quantity to provide for the number of classes scheduled each period without exceeding the normal class size.

CLASS ORGANIZATION AND MANAGEMENT THROUGH ACTIVITY

Research and practice clearly indicate teachers who organize and manage their classes through activity—***keeping all students actively engaged and successful***—not only have an easier time managing instructional time and student behavior, but also have students learning at higher levels. Teachers must not only plan for this type of activity, but must also take time to teach students routines and how to take responsibility to use equipment, participate in instruction and practice, and move around the facility in an appropriate manner.

If students, at any level, are taught appropriate rules and procedures and are given the responsibility to manage themselves within that structure, they will respond appropriately. The following tips will provide an outline for successful class organization and management through student activity.

Beginning Class

As noted earlier in this section, students come to physical education prepared for activity. Therefore, the tone of the lesson must be established as soon as the students enter the facility. The amount of time typically spent at the beginning of the class for "administrative or managerial" tasks often slows or stops the pace of the lesson and simply turns off the students' desire to be active. One way to get things moving and to reduce the amount of "administrative" time is to post information regarding what students are expected to do when entering the facility.

The information should be posted in a place visible to all students upon entering the facility. If the students need to change clothes, a spot in the locker room near the exit door to the gymnasium works great. If the students come straight to the facility without changing clothes, having a bulletin board visible upon entering is recommended. The information should include what students should do upon entering the facility and what activity will be presented during the day. At the elementary level another great idea is to have the classroom teacher post a weekly schedule of activities on the bulletin board. This way the students know what to expect for the week and can anticipate the activities.

Sample Informational Posting

DAY: MONDAY   **CLASS:** This can either be individuals classes or grouped according to the levels. (eg: Jones, Smith, and Roe or 3–5

Challenge Stations:
　　Go to "challenge station" of your choice
　　Be prepared to record your score when asked

Fitness Core: Aerobic Routine "America"
Leaders: Jonathan, Brad and Taylor
Find your own space and be ready to begin

Core Activity: Volleyball Serve
Formation: semi-circle at north end
5 stations with activities; 5 minutes/station
We will complete 3–5 stations today

Game: Partner Frisbee Tag
Form groups of three (3) w/in 30 seconds

By letting students know what is expected, they will have the opportunity to prepare and think about what they must do—they take the responsibility for management. With this procedure teachers are not required to take away from instructional time to give simple directions.

Another positive method of organization and management of activity is to "teach for signal attention." This also must be done at the beginning of the year or semester. Time is most often wasted when teachers attempt to get the attention of the entire class and fail. There are many methods of gaining attention—a whistle, stopping music, clapping hands, etc. Whichever method is used students must be taught what to do when the signal is given. To teach students the proper response to your signal, first clearly identify what is expected; practice by giving the signal at various times throughout the class, giving positive feedback when the proper response is given. By using high rates of feedback and positive individual/class interactions, students will respond quickly and appropriately.

Finally, keep the class period flowing. As the lesson moves from one component to the next, keep the transition time quick and smooth. If, during the instructional/practice component, you notice the tempo slowing, stop the students and have them participate in a "Quickie Fitness Activity" as noted in Section 2. By providing a change in tempo and activity, students are kept active and involved at all times. The majority of discipline problems occurring in physical education are due to lack of active participation and individual student success. In order to maintain these two essential components, the lesson must be moving forward at a challenging level throughout the class period.

INSTRUCTIONAL SUCCESS

The major difference in today's physical education lies in its student-centered and success-oriented instructional approach. Large amounts of self-direction have been incorporated into the approach as contrasted with former teacher-centered strategies. The current program should guarantee each student maximal involvement in physically active experiences.

Different styles of teaching should be utilized, ranging from teacher-led to student-directed or individualized. The problem-solving method becomes an important instructional approach. In the elementary grades, attention is centered on the development of body management and movement, and competency in basic skills,

while the focus shifts to the development of more specialized skills at the intermediate level. This places more emphasis on movement exploration in the primary grades and a variety of instructional procedures for intermediate/middle-level students. These approaches include the use of task cards, levels approaches, journals, etc. (See Sections 2, 3, and 4.)

Curricular content should be organized so learning takes place in a sequential manner. There must be enough time allocated to tasks so skills are "mastered" at developmentally appropriate levels and students learn not only the "what and how" but the "why" of each activity and how it promotes the development and maintenance of a healthy lifestyle.

SUCCESS FOR STUDENTS WITH SPECIAL NEEDS

Today, physical educators will have students with various special needs in their classes. These individuals might be there for selected units of the class, be assisted by an aide, or be fully integrated. If there are questions or concerns about including these students in classes or their particular needs, contact should be made with an adapted physical education specialist, a special education teacher, the parent, or the students themselves.

In terms of including these students in classes, some modifications may have to be made to allow for successful participation. Simply put, there are three main areas/activities in physical education that can be modified to meet the individual needs of each student: the instruction, the environment, and the activity.

Modifying Instruction

The goal of instructional modification is to enhance communication between teacher and student, with special attention given to ensuring communication with the special needs student. The following modifications are suggested.

1. Language—simple words, demonstrations, one-step directions
2. Making concepts concrete—be extremely clear
3. Sequencing tasks—teach using "small" steps
4. Extending time—provide more practice time
5. Expanding the use of the senses—auditory-visual, auditory-tactile, visual-kinesthetic, etc.

Modifying the Environment

To enhance learning, it sometimes becomes necessary to modify the learning environment to better meet students' educational needs. Some suggestions are:

1. Modify the facility—ramps, adjusted goals/boundaries
2. Use space creatively—reduced areas of activity, stations
3. Eliminate distractions—keep attention focused
4. Provide structure—teach and keep a structured routine

Modifying the Activity

Any physical activity can be modified. Modification should be made for the purposes of inclusion and participation of *all* students in the class, including those with special needs. Modifications should be done with the participation and learning experience of all students in mind. The following techniques should be considered:

1. Individual placement—safety, mobility, peer teaching
2. Time of participation—consideration of health impairments
3. Equipment—make use of individual abilities, vary color, length, weight, etc.
4. Rules—change as part of the instructional process, don't change so much that the game itself is lost

Physical education programs for individuals with special needs can be fun and should not be feared or avoided. A willingness to attempt to understand the abilities and limitations of those with disabilities and to include special needs students are the two key ingredients to a successful program. Including special needs students in physical activity isn't always difficult nor is it always different, but it is always meaningful to *all active and successful participants.*

GENERAL GUIDELINES FOR STUDENT SAFETY

Student safety is a major consideration throughout the school system. Within the physical education program, safety is promoted through planning and implementation placing emphasis on the needs and abilities of students. Competent leadership, suitable equipment, and facilities that are maintained in a safe and usable condition are priorities. For example:

1. Activities should only be undertaken after instruction has been given.
2. Students are aware of all safety precautions involving each activity.

3. Students are assigned to practice activities within their proven capabilities.

4. Equipment should only be used when the instructor is assured of its safe condition.

5. Proper documentation indicating teaching progression and techniques have been utilized.

In the event of student injury, care must be taken to provide appropriate treatment as determined by local school policy and procedure. It is the responsibility of each teacher to maintain appropriate documentation of all situations in which a student is injured and to maintain a current knowledge of emergency-care procedures and techniques.

The following concepts should be taken into consideration when planning and implementing a sound program:

1. Allow students to progress at their own pace while encouraging active participation in new activities.

2. In relays or other running activities, students should not use a wall to stop their movement or for changing directions.

3. Students should be reminded to always "watch where they are going" and to be aware of others.

4. Activities involving "heavy" contact should be avoided.

5. Mats should be placed under *all* pieces of apparatus that involve activities taking place above the ground.

6. When "pairing" students, place students of like size/ability together.

7. Keep *all* movement patterns away from equipment in use or other student activity.

8. *Always* provide students with safety procedures prior to participation and check that they know the procedures.

9. *Always* be aware of all student activity and be in a position to respond appropriately to any situation.

STUDENT-CENTERED EQUIPMENT

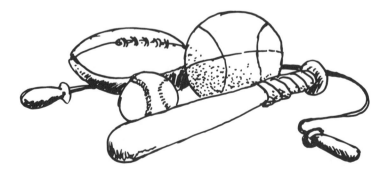

The availability of suitable equipment in appropriate quantity is essential to the implementation of a quality physical education program. The following list provides suggestions for minimal equipment needs.

Sample Equipment for Grades 1-5

$8\frac{1}{2}''$ to 10″ rubber playground balls

beanbags

hula hoops

36″ cage ball

sponge rubber and junior footballs

junior basketballs

baskets at different heights—6′ to 10′

pinnies/vests

floor hockey sticks

unicycles

7′ to 8′ jump ropes

sets of 16′ double-dutch jump ropes

flying discs

sponge rubber and soft softballs

right- and left-handed softball gloves

softball masks

plastic wiffleballs

plastic bats

softball aluminum bats

batting tees

wood paddles, paddle balls

sponge rubber and junior soccer balls

tether balls

scooters

stilts

cone boundary markers

parachute (large)

volleyball nets and stands

volleyballs—trainers and regular leather

rubber gym bases

pogo sticks

juggling cubes and scarves

footbags

tape player and speaker system

100′ tape measure

electric pump

beach balls

balloons

chin bars

bounce boards

low balance beams

individual tug-of-war ropes

36″ hardwood dowels (wands)

4 × 8 folding mats

5 × 10 crash pad

Sample Equipment for Grades 6-8

flying discs

footbags

cycles (unicycle, bicycle, circus cycles, etc.)

sponge rubber balls (footballs, soccer balls)

soccer balls

footballs

volleyballs—trainers and regular leather

basketballs—junior and regular

pinnies/vests

juggling—cubes, clubs, scarves, boxes, flick sticks, rings, etc.

7′ to 9′ jump ropes

16′ double-dutch ropes

Chinese jump ropes

pogo sticks

gym scooter

stilts

parachute

bowling set

tennis balls (indoor, soft, regular)

36″ cage ball

hula hoops

wands

rackets—tennis, pickleball, paddleball, racquetball

nets—volleyball, tennis, badminton, pickleball

floor hockey sets

golf clubs and practice balls

track and field equipment

roller skates

deck tennis rings

tape player and speaker system

4 × 8 folding mats

5 × 10 crash pad

archery sets

weights—free weights, cable machines, dumbbells

aerobic equipment—stationary cycles, rowing machines, etc.

body composition measurement instrument

heart rate monitors

electric ball pump

CONCLUSION

In the final analysis, it is the realization of the mind-body relationship that now stimulates physical education to make a significant contribution to the total development of each individual student. If we wish to educate our children through physical movement, we must create a learning environment that stimulates students to think and to become aware of what their bodies can do. Each student needs opportunities to explore, experiment, create, and select movement patterns suitable for his or her needs. The student further needs to consolidate his or her skills with appropriate practice. This may mean de-emphasizing the highly competitive situations and eliminating the frustration wherein the student fails and may eliminate physical activity from his or her life.

2
Fitness Activities

SECTION 2

Fitness Activities

In contrast to the programs presented at the primary-grade levels, emphasis during the intermediate grades and at the middle level shift towards a more formalized approach to exercise patterns and activities. Correct fitness concepts, exercise techniques, and safety considerations must be presented to and mastered by all students as they progress.

In order to provide an interesting program and increase the individual motivation, exercise activities should be varied and include personal challenges on a daily basis. The focus of activities presented in this section is to increase student interest and motivation while at the same time providing a variety of challenging ways to enhance physical-fitness levels. As students progress and the year moves forward, less instructional time will be necessary as the students become familiar with the individual skills and activities, thus providing increased opportunity to interact with students while providing for individual needs and prescriptive assistance.

Each of the activities presented is designed to develop and enhance individual fitness levels. Some activities will emphasize total body fitness, some will isolate specific components, while still others will combine motor skills and fitness components. Together this approach allows for variations based on individuals, facilities, equipment, and scheduling formats.

As will be noted, the majority of activities are performed for a specific period of time rather than a specific number of repetitions. This format provides students with the opportunity to exercise at an individual intensity level rather than a predetermined level. Utilizing this format, individual students will have a better chance of success and will be able to monitor their progress.

As with most of us, some students will need to be motivated to work harder and others will be looking for greater challenges. The design of these activities allows for both ranges and for all students to experience success each day.

EXERCISE ACTIVITY DESCRIPTIONS

Here is a written description of each exercise/activity discussed in this guide. As you introduce each general routine, refer to this listing if necessary.

Arm Circle

Stand with feet together, arms out to side with palms down. (With or without weights.) Circle both arms forward simultaneously in 12-inch circles. Circle both arms backward simultaneously in 12-inch circles. **(upper body)**

Bend and Stretch

Stand with hands on hips, feet slightly apart. Keeping knees slightly bent, bend forward at hips, keeping back flat. Hold this position for 20 to 25 seconds, stand up, and repeat. (**warm-up**)

Bicycle

Lying on backs, two students extend legs, hands under hips. Lift legs to a vertical position above hips. Arms may support back. To begin bicycling motion, students alternately bend and straighten legs at knee. (**warm-up**)

Body Bender

Stand with feet slightly apart, hands clasped overhead with palms up. Slowly bend sideward at hips to the left as far as possible. Keeping feet stationary and toes pointed straight forward, return to starting position. Repeat, bending to the right, repeat to the front (don't round the back). Return to the starting position. **(flexibility)**

Body Twist

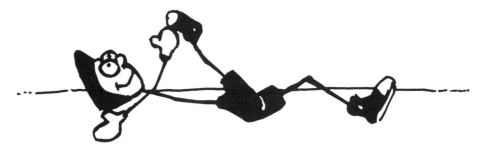

Lie on back, arms extended sideward, palms on the floor. Slowly swing the left leg up and across the body touching the floor near the right hand. Keep arms, shoulders, and head in contact with the floor, hold for 10 seconds and return to the starting position. Repeat swinging the right leg to the left side.

Chair/Bench Dip

Place hands on front of a chair or bench, extend feet in front, knees straight. From this support position, lower body until shoulder and elbow form a 90-degree angle. Raise up

until arms are straight and repeat. *Variation:* Support feet on a chair/bench at the same level as the support for hands. **(upper body, abdominal)**

Crab Walk

Assume a "rear" support position with the hands directly under the shoulders and fingers facing away from the feet. From this position "walk" forward, backward or to either side.

Crab Dip

From the crab walk position bend arms at the elbow, lowering the body approximately 2 inches from the ground. Push up to the full support position.

Crab Kick

Start in crab walk position. (The body is supported on hands and feet with the back to the floor and knees bent at approximately a 45-degree angle; bend elbow slightly.) Lift right leg forward and up, hold for 10 seconds. Bring right leg back to starting position and repeat with left leg forward. (**upper body**)

Crunch

While lying on a mat, fold arms across chest, lift legs off the ground with knees bent to form a 90-degree angle. Lift head and shoulders off the mat, return, and repeat. *Variation:* Place lower legs on a chair with hips on the ground directly in front of the chair. (**abdominal**)

Curl-Up

Lie on back with feet flat and knees bent. Place hands on opposite shoulders so that the arms cross the chest. Lift head and upper body off the mat, return, and repeat. (**abdominal**)

Half Curl-Up

Lie on back with knees bent, feet flat, and hands flat on the top of thighs. Slide hands forward until fingers touch top of knee caps, lifting head, shoulders, and upper body from floor. Hold for two or more counts. Return to starting position. **(abdominal)**

Frisky Pony Kick

With arms straight at shoulder and eyes focused on the hands, lift legs up toward a handstand position. Then kick up and out with the legs before completing a full handstand. **(upper body, lower body)**

Heel Slap/Knee Tap

Stand, arms held at the side. Lift left foot up and behind the right knee, touching left foot with right hand. Repeat, lifting right foot behind left knee to touch right foot with left hand. Lift right knee and touch with left hand; lift left knee, touch with right hand. Repeat entire motion (foot/foot/knee/knee). **(warm-up)**

Kick Through

In push-up position, support weight on hands and toes. Bring right leg under the body toward left hand. At the same time, raise left arm off the ground to shoulder height. Continue the leg upward until the foot and hand meet. Hold for 10 seconds, return to starting position, and repeat the motion to lift left foot to right hand. **(upper body, flexibility)**

Lateral Stretch

From front straddle position, point toes straight ahead, keep back straight, and bend right knee forward. **(lower body)**

Push-Up

Extend arms and place hands on ground just under and slightly outside of shoulders, fingers pointing forward. Extend body so that it is perfectly straight. (The weight is supported on the hands and toes.) Keeping body tense and straight, bend elbows and touch chest to floor. Return to original position. Care must be taken to assure proper body alignment: keep body straight; buttocks not raised and abdomen not sagging. **(upper body)**

Push-Up Variations

All push-ups begin from a front support position (except "Spider" push-ups).

Triangle Push-Up   Hands are placed directly under mid-chest with thumb and first finger of each hand touching (thumb at right angles to the finger, wrists rotated slightly inward). Lower the body to the hands and raise up.

Wide Spread Push-Up   Place hands on the floor out from the shoulder. Make distances progressively wider depending on the strength of the student.

Push and Clap   This exercise should be done on a mat and only with students of sufficient strength and coordination. From the "down" position, thrust body upward. While body is in the air, clap the hands together, move apart, and "catch" the body prior to touching the ground.

Fingertip Push-Up   Similar to a regular push-up except the body is supported on the fingertips instead of having the palms flat on the floor. This activity can also be done using any of the other suggested push-up variations. Push up with the arms and

legs while, at the same time, moving into a back arch position. Hold for a few seconds, then return to starting position, ready to repeat the movement.

Line Push-Up Assume a push-up position with hands placed in front of a horizontal line on the floor. When raising body up from the down position, "walk" the hands behind the line. During the next "up" phase, "walk" the hands back in front of the line.

Elevated Push-Up Assume a push-up position with the feet elevated on either a bench or a chair. From that position perform either a regular push-up or any variation.

Reclining Pull-Up (Partner Pull-Up) Lie on the back, with partner standing astride looking face-to-face, feet beside reclining student's chest. Partners grasp hands, with fingers interlocked. Reclining student's arms are fully extended. Student on the floor pulls up with arms until chest touches partner's thighs, with the body remaining straight, weight resting on heels. The standing partner supports but does not aid action. Return to starting position and repeat.

Quad Stretch

From front straddle position, bend front knee to a 90-degree angle. At the same time bend back leg to a 90-degree angle towards the floor. Hold a position with the back leg approximately 3 inches from the floor. **(lower body)**

Rowing

Lie on back with arms extended over head. Sit up and reach forward with extended arms, while pulling the knees against the chest. Arms are outside the knees. Return to starting position and repeat. **(abdominal)**

Side Flex

From a standing position extend the right arm over the head with the left arm crossed in front of the body. Slowly bend to the left, hold for 10 seconds. Repeat with the left arm overhead and the right arm crossed in front.

Squat Thrust

Stand in an erect position. Bend knees and place hands on floor in front of feet. (Arms in front of the bent knees.) Thrust legs back far enough so that the body is straight from shoulders to feet (the push-up position). Care must be taken to assure proper alignment of knees and back when in the extended position. (**muscular strength, endurance**)

Treadmill

Assume push-up position with one leg brought forward so that the knee is under the chest. Remain in this position while legs are moved in a rhythmic running pattern. (**muscular strength, endurance**)

Trunk Twister

Stand with feet 24 inches apart, hands clasped behind head, elbows held backward. Slowly bend downward, knees slightly bent and back flat. Simultaneously rotate trunk to left. Same to the right. Return to original position. (**flexibility**)

Twist and Bend

Stand with feet spread shoulder-width apart, knees slightly bent, arms extended over-head, and hands interlocked. Slowly twist the trunk to the right while bending forward and touching the floor *inside* the right foot with the fingers of both hands. Hold for 10 seconds. Keep trunk and hands down and touch floor outside the toes of the right foot. Hold for 10 seconds. Repeat, touching *outside* and *heel* of the right foot. Return to starting position, sweeping trunk and arms upward in a wide arc, twisting to the left and touching the left foot. Continue, alternating to each side. **(flexibility)**

V-Sit and Reach

Start in sitting position, with legs extended forward, knees slightly bent, feet approximately 24 inches apart. Keeping the back straight, slowly bend at the waist and reach forward with the arms as far as possible. *Hold the full bent position for 10 seconds.* Return to starting position and repeat. **(abdominal)**

V Sit-Up

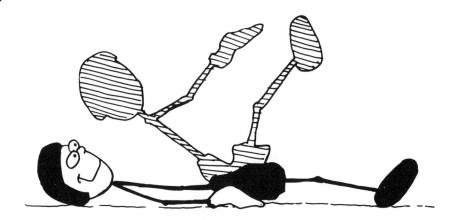

Lie on back, arms at sides with palms down. Simultaneously raise trunk forward and upward, and legs upward. Grasp lower legs and hold position for 10 seconds. Return to starting position and repeat. **(abdominal)**

Wall Sit

Stand with back flat against a wall. Keeping the back flat against the wall, lower body until knees have reached a 90-degree angle. Hold this position for specified length of time. **(lower body)**

Wing Stretcher

Stand in erect position and raise elbows to shoulder height, palms down, in front of chest. Move elbows backward. Hold for 10 seconds. Bring elbows forward as far as possible. Hold for 10 seconds. **(upper body)**

ANIMAL WALK CIRCUIT (K-1)

Focus: Muscular strength, endurance, flexibility

Equipment: Prepared cards

Description:

A low-organized activity using various animal movements to increase fitness levels and movement patterns.

Procedure:

On colored sheets of $8\frac{1}{2} \times 11$ paper, write the names of various animal walks and/or draw a picture of the movements/animal. Randomly place the cards around the facility. Have the students move to open areas and get ready to move.

1. On the start signal, all students begin to "Kangaroo Jump" around the facility.
2. On the stop signal, students move to the nearest card and begin to perform the animal walk listed towards the next card.
3. Upon reaching the next card, the students change to the animal walk noted and move to another card.
4. This rotation continues for 60 seconds. After that time, students begin to "Kangaroo Jump" for 30 seconds.
5. This cycle can be repeated depending on the physical ability of the students.

Modification:

Eliminate the "Kangaroo Jump" at the beginning of the activity. Have students move directly to an activity card and begin to move from card to card using the appropriate animal movement.

COLOR CHALLENGE CIRCUIT (K-2)

Focus: Fitness development and movement competency

Equipment: Hoops, task cards

Description:

A series of movement-oriented task cards is placed in hula hoops spaced randomly around the facility. Students alternate locomotor activities and activities from each task card.

Procedure:

Place different colored hula hoops or other markers randomly around the facility. Inside each hoop or beside each marker, place colored task cards.

1. On signal, students begin a locomotor activity moving randomly around the facility.
2. On the stop signal, students move to the nearest task card and perform the listed activity for 15 seconds.
3. After completing that activity, they begin a selected locomotor activity for 30 seconds, stop on signal, and perform a different challenge.

Sample Activities:

1. PINK: Touch your elbow to the floor, then hop on your right foot ten times, then hop on your left foot ten times.
2. GREEN: Touch your right knee to the floor, then do 15 curl-ups or modified curl-ups.
3. YELLOW: Sit down and stand up 20 times.
4. ORANGE: Put your hands on the floor and do 15 "Frisky Pony Kicks."
5. GRAY: Make a bridge and wave to four friends with your right hand, shake your left foot in the air five times, then wave to four different friends.
6. WHITE: Jump back and forth over a line 20 times.

EXERCISE LINES (K–2)

Focus: General fitness and coordination

Equipment: None

Description:

These low-organized, fast-moving exercise routines provide a challenge along with variations on traditional themes to increase student motivation and increase activity levels.

Procedure:

Divide students into three groups: upper body strength—cardiovascular endurance—abdominal strength. Have each group form a line with students approximately arms' distance apart. Assign each group a specific exercise to do within the specified time limit.

1. Exercises are performed by all group members for the time limit.
2. After the time limit has expired, students stand, jog for 30 seconds, and come back to their line and prepare for the next exercise.
3. After completing all exercises, students jog for 30 seconds and walk for another 30 seconds.

Modification:

Determine the number of repetitions and exercise activities based on the ability and fitness levels of students.

Sample Activities:

1. *Upper Body Strength:* Duration 30 seconds. From push-up position move one hand at a time back and forth over a line as fast as possible. Keep knees off the ground and back straight.
2. *Cardiovascular Endurance:* Duration 30 seconds. Keeping feet together jump forward and back as many times as possible. Try jumping side to side.
3. *Abdominal Strength:* Duration 30 seconds. Do line beanbag curl-ups: Sit up as far as you can; hold the up position and pass a beanbag under your leg to the person on your right. After passing the beanbag, keep "curling-up" as many times as you can. When the beanbag reaches the end of the line, start passing it back.

I-CAN-DO-IT MOTIVATIONAL CARDS (K-2)

Focus: Simple task cards and immediate rewards to provide goals and motivation

Equipment: Task cards, equipment as needed

Description:

Personal motivation is the key to success in any activity. In order to challenge and motivate students to achieve at higher levels, goals should be established and rewards given. The use of simple task cards designed to provide practice and challenges are provided. These tasks should be used as a basis for your planning—design your own cards based on student interests and abilities.

Procedure:

Duplicate primary "Challenge Cards" onto an $8\frac{1}{2} \times 11$ colored sheet of paper and laminate. Post all, or a portion of the cards, on the walls throughout the facility. Have students work on these challenges periodically during the week. In addition to the wall-mounted challenge cards, make individual "reward cards" and give them to students when challenges are met.

1. Periodically give students a "fitness challenge" break. During this 5-minute break, students work at various stations trying to complete the challenge.
2. If a student is successful, they receive the "I Can Do It" motivational card corresponding with the task.
3. Once a student has earned all cards, let the student attempt a "personal record" at each station.

Organization:

The following cards should be modified to meet individual ability and fitness levels of your class. If challenge levels are set too high, students will become frustrated and fail to attempt the challenge.

I CAN JUMP

TIMES IN
60 SECONDS

I CAN DO A

FRONT CROSS WITH
MY JUMP ROPE

I CAN DO A

BACK CROSS WITH
MY JUMP ROPE

I CAN DO 10

CONTINUOUS CROSSES
WITH MY JUMP ROPE

I CAN JUMP BACKWARDS FOR ONE MINUTE

WITH LESS THAN THREE MISSES

I CAN DO FIVE

DOUBLE UNDERS WITHOUT A MISS

I CAN JUMP ROPE FOR ONE MINUTE

WITH LESS THAN THREE MISSES

I CAN PERFORM

3 BASIC JUMP ROPE SKILLS

I CAN DO

60 SECONDS OF CONTINUOUS ROWING

I CAN DO

30 SECONDS OF CONTINUOUS ROWING

I CAN DO _____

CURL-UPS IN 60 SECONDS

I CAN DO 25

CHAIR CRUNCHES

I CAN JOG A MILE

I CAN JOG A MILE

IN 9 MINUTES

IN 10 MINUTES

I CAN DO 50

I CAN DO 10 REPETITIONS

JUMPS IN AND OUT OF A HOOP

OF THE SHUTTLE RUN

I CAN PERFORM

A HANDSTAND

I CAN DO THE
BAR HANG

FOR _____
SECONDS

I CAN CLIMB TO
THE TOP

OF THE ROPE

I CAN DO

_____

PULL-UPS

I CAN DO 30
SECONDS

OF CONTINUOUS
MT. CLIMBERS

I CAN DO 10
CONTINUOUS

REPETITIONS OF
THE BALL HOP

I CAN RUN 10

LAPS OF THE GYM

I CAN JUMP
ROPE FOR

2 MINUTES

I CAN DO
10

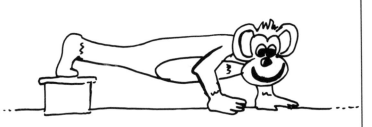

ELEVATED PUSH-UPS
(feet on a bench)

I CAN DO
10

CRAB DIPS
(with hands on
a chair)

I CAN DO
30 SECONDS

OF CONTINUOUS
CRAB WALK

I CAN DO
15

PUSH-UPS

KEEP MOVING (K-2)

Focus: General fitness development

Equipment: None

Description:

Students walk/jog in a circle. Students are chosen in rapid succession to go to the center and become leaders.

Procedure:

Have students walk/jog in a circle formation at the center of the facility. Select one student to move to the center and become the leader. When the leader goes to the center, all students stop moving forward, turn to the center, and keep walking in place.

1. The center leader keeps his or her feet moving and performs any movement as long as the feet keep moving. The students in the circle perform the same movements as the leader.
2. After 15 seconds, the leader goes back to the circle and all students begin the walk/jog.
3. After 15 seconds of the walk/jog, a new leader is picked to go to the center and begin his or her movements.

Organization:

1. Keep students moving rapidly and encourage innovative movements from all leaders.
2. Keep the group going until all students have had the opportunity to be leaders. You may have to shorten the time involved for each leader.

LATERALITY FITNESS (K-2)

Focus: Fitness and coordination skills; patterning, movement, and general fitness development

Equipment: None

Description:

Exercises and activities are grouped as bilateral (using both sides of the body at the same time), unilateral (using one side of the body at a time), and cross-lateral (crossing the midline). Emphasis is placed on each exercise/activity group for a period of six weeks. At the end of this time period, students move to the next series. During the final six weeks of the school year, students should take part in a combination of all exercises/activities.

Procedure:

Space students randomly around the facility. After demonstrating the exercise/activity, have students follow you (or leader) through the progression.

Bilateral

—Both sides of the body moving at the same time. Go slowly so that students can concentrate on proper movement and form.

1. *Body Awareness:* Hold each position for 10 seconds. Touch shoulders, knees, hips, toes, ankles, heels, ears, nose. Repeat in any order. Go faster as students gain in ability.
2. Random hopping around the room (a hop is on both feet).
3. *Angels in the Snow:* Go slowly at first, placing emphasis on moving both arms and legs at the same time. More skilled students do jumping jacks.
4. *Arm Movements:* Move both arms at the same time. Lift up, put to the side, small circles, large circles, to the front, down, up high, circle, forward, up, etc.
5. *Knee Push-Ups:* Use proper form by extending the body forward. If a student has trouble doing a push-up, have him or her hold a position halfway down for a few seconds, then go back up.
6. *Half or Whole Curl-Up:* With arms across the chest or at the side, have the students curl-up. It is okay if the students can only lift their head off the ground.
7. *Bunny Hops:* Randomly perform bunny hops (jumps) around the room.
8. *Stand and Stretch:* Reach as high up in the air as possible and hold the position. Go up on toes and balance.

Unilateral

—Using one side of the body at a time. Emphasis should be placed on holding the "nonmoving" side still while the other side is moving. The teacher may have to help students by holding the "nonmoving" side.

1. *Body Awareness:* Same as in bilateral only using one arm at a time.
2. *Angels in the Snow:* Move only one side of the body at a time. More skilled students do one-sided jumping jacks.
3. *Bear Walk:* Randomly do a Bear Walk around the room.
4. *Side Leg Lifts:* Lying on their side with the hand supporting the head, have the students lift their top leg up and down. Hold the "up" position for approximately five to ten seconds. Roll over and repeat with the other leg.
5. *Knee Lift Curls:* From a curl-up position, with knees bent and right hand on the right shoulder, have the students lift their head off the ground and bring the right knee to the right elbow. Repeat 10 to 15 times and switch to the left side.
6. *Gallop Around the Room:* Perform for one to two minutes, switching lead legs at the halfway point.
7. *Coffee Grinder:* From a side-lean position, supporting the body with either the right or left arm and the same foot, have the student move in a circle around the supporting arm.
8. *Hop on One Foot:* Try to stay in one place. Change foot after 10 to 15 seconds.

Cross-lateral

—Crossing over the body midline with movement; e.g., using right arm and left foot.

1. *Body Awareness:* Touch left side with right hand and right side with left hand. Do one hand at a time.
2. *Angels in the Snow:* Move right arm and left leg, then left arm and right leg. More skilled students do cross-over jumping jacks.
3. *Crab Walk:* Randomly do a Crab Walk around the facility.
4. *Alternate Leg Lifts:* Lying on their back, have students lift their leg—knee slightly bent—into the air at the same time they lift their opposite arm. Have them touch their foot to their hand.
5. *Knee Lift Curls:* Same as in bilateral only have them touch the knee to the opposite elbow.
6. *Skip Around the Room:* Concentrate on having the arm movements be opposite the leg movement; e.g., when the right foot is forward the left hand should be forward.
7. *Kick Through:* From a front support position (push-up position), have the students bring their right leg under their body and touch their left hand. Repeat to the opposite side. For a challenge lift the arm into the air, twist, balance, and touch.
8. *Random Running:* Run around the facility at different speeds.

Motivation:

1. Change speeds—first go slowly, then quickly, then back to slow.
2. Make a challenge—individual or group—by saying "Can you do a certain number?" or "How high can you jump?"
3. Play music.
4. Do these activities at various times during the physical education period.
5. Have the classroom teacher follow-up by having a PE challenge using these activities in the classroom.
6. Give small certificates if a student improves, can do an activity without assistance, or can do all the activities without a "miss."
7. Have students face in a different direction or move to a different location for each exercise/activity.

PRIMARY NUMBER CHALLENGE (K-2)

Focus: General fitness development

Equipment: Number cards

Description:

Students choose three different exercises and perform the repetitions corresponding to the numbers shown by the teacher.

Procedure:

Begin students in a scatter formation around the facility. Hold a group discussion prior to the activity to share possible activities that could be used to meet the challenges. Display a series of numbers (the numbers should also be verbally presented). Have the students respond by performing various exercise/activities with repetitions determined by the numbers shown.

1. Students begin to slowly jog around the facility in a random manner.
2. On signal the students stop, look for the challenge numbers, and begin to exercise. EXAMPLE:

> Numbers 5-3-6
>
> 5 jumping jacks
>
> 3 curl-up/modifications
>
> 6 coffee grinders

3. After several sets the students jog for 30 seconds and walk for another 30 seconds.

Motivation:

Encourage students to try different exercise/activities.

RANDOM PRIMARY CIRCUITS (K-2)

Focus: Flexibility, cardiovascular, muscular strength

Equipment: None

Description:

A low-organized set of fitness activities intermixed with fast-moving locomotor movements.

Procedure:

Using a random formation, have students begin to move using different locomotor movements. Each student can choose a different movement or the entire group can do the same movement. At the conclusion of one minute, have all students stop moving and perform a fitness activity for 15 seconds (possibly 30 seconds for older students).

1. Fitness activities include stretching, jumping jacks, modified curl-ups, modified push-ups, crab kicks, and laterality activities. (See "Laterality Fitness.")

2. After performing the fitness activity for 20 seconds, students resume locomotor activities for 15 seconds, then perform another activity.

3. At the conclusion of all activities, students should finish with 1 minute of slow jogging, followed by 30 seconds of walking.

BASIC TEACHER/LEADER EXERCISES (K-8)

Focus: Flexibility, muscular strength/endurance, cardiovascular

Equipment: Jump ropes

Description:

A predetermined set of specific exercises performed by students and lead by either the teacher or student.

Procedure:

Space students around the facility either in a scatter formation, per set lines, a circle, or other organizational pattern so that each student may see the leader. If the exercises are new to the students, a demonstration will be necessary.

1. Go through the exercises, including at least one activity from each fitness component group.
2. Do each exercise activity for a predetermined amount of time and allow students to use individual variations so that they experience the greatest benefit.

Motivation and Challenges:

1. Have various students lead during each class period.
2. Play music during the activity.
3. Move to each student and challenge him or her to do a different variation of the exercise/activity or to do more.
4. Have one leader in each quadrant of the facility and rotate the one leading with each exercise/activity. Have students turn and face the new leader.

Sample Routine:

EXERCISE	ACTIVITY DURATION (BEG./INT./ADV.)		
Bend and Stretch	20 sec	25 sec	30 sec
Trunk Twist	10 rep	12 rep	15 rep
Arm Circles	30 sec	30 sec	30 sec
Rope Skipping	45 sec	60 sec	90 sec
Push-Ups (variations)	30 sec	35 sec	40 sec
Running in Place	45 sec	60 sec	90 sec
Crab Kicks	30 sec	40 sec	60 sec
Treadmill	45 sec	60 sec	90 sec
Curl-Ups (variations)	30 sec	35 sec	40 sec
Jogging Perimeter	90 sec	2 min	4 min
Walking Cool-Down	1 min	1 min	1 min

THE 2-MINUTE DRILL (K–8)

Focus: Increase overall fitness levels

Equipment: None

Description:

This activity is a good, quick fitness motivator to use in the middle of a slower paced activity or at the beginning of a class period. Classroom teachers can also use it for a break during classroom activities.

Procedure:

Have the students find an open space. On signal they each take their pulse for 6 seconds and add a "0" to get their beginning rate.

1. On the start signal, students begin the first activity as directed by the teacher/leader. This activity lasts for 15 seconds.
2. After 15 seconds, they begin the second activity.
3. Continue this rotation for a total of 8 activities.
4. At the completion of 2 minutes, have the students take their pulse rate again and note the difference.
5. Cool-down by walking for 1 minute.

Organization:

Do not give the students a break between activities. This should be continuous exercise for the entire 2 minutes.

Sample Activities:

Jumping Jacks	Jog in Place	Push-Ups
Curl-Ups	Treadmills	Kick Through
Crab Kicks	Sit and Reach	Jump Rope
Chair Dips	Animal Walks	Crunches

SPACE RUN (1-8)

Focus: Cardiovascular endurance, muscular strength, flexibility

Equipment: None

Description:

A challenging aerobic activity interspersed with vigorous exercise activities, done without specific equipment and can be done equally indoors or out.

Procedure:

Arrange students around the perimeter of the facility about 5 to 7 feet apart. Have all students begin a slow jog in a clockwise direction keeping their spacing.

1. While jogging give the signal to stop and direct all students to begin performing a specific exercise. (Allow students to use individual variations based on their skill and fitness levels.)
2. Once the exercise set is completed, students begin to jog again.
3. Continue until all exercise activities have been completed and finish with a 1-minute jog and 1-minute walk.

Organization and Modifications:

1. If students want to pass the person in front of them, have them move to the "outside" and pass.
2. Choose a minimum of two activities from each fitness component group to begin with and increase as fitness levels increase.

Sample Activities and Format:

(intermediate level)

Jog	60 seconds	Half Curl	30 seconds
Body Bender	30 seconds	Jog	60 seconds
Jog	60 seconds	Heel Slap	30 seconds
Crab Kick	30 seconds	Jog	60 seconds
Jog	60 seconds	Push-Up	30 seconds
Kick Through	30 seconds	Jog	2 minutes
Jog	60 seconds		

TREASURE HUNT (1-8)

Focus: Overall fitness

Equipment: Task cards, equipment as determined by tasks

Description:

A free-style exercise activity with all students performing different exercises as indicated by cards they pick up from a stack placed in the center of the facility.

Procedure:

Develop a group of task cards listing specific fitness activities and motor skills. Place the cards in the center of the facility and have all students scatter around, making certain they each have an individual space.

1. On the start signal, all students run and take an exercise card and go to their space to perform the activity as listed.
2. When they have completed the activity, they return the card to the center and take another.
3. The activity continues for a designated time period; e.g., beginners, 5 minutes; intermediates, 7 minutes; advanced, 10 minutes.

Organization and Modifications:

1. Place the tasks on 3 × 5 cards and laminate.
2. Tell students not to read the cards until they have returned to their space.
3. Change the cards over a period of time to reflect student interest and ability.
4. If motor skills are being used, have specific areas of those activities and place the necessary equipment in that area.
5. Instead of returning the cards to the center, have students exchange the cards with others until each student has done a specific number of activities. (Tell students they must always exchange with a different person—it's okay for them to repeat activities.)
6. To accommodate individual reading levels, have students work with partners.
7. When using this activity with grades 1 and 2, the individual cards should include a picture of the activity as well as a written task.
8. Keep the tasks simple and modify for ability and developmental levels in the primary grades.

Sample Challenges:

1. Jog around the facility 2 times.
2. Do 5 Push-Ups in each quadrant of the facility.
3. Jump Rope 25 times using a jogging step.

4. Hop the length of the facility with a ball between your legs.
5. Do 15 Kick Throughs.
6. Perform 5 Curl-Ups in each quadrant of the facility.
7. Crab Walk 30 feet.
8. Do 50 Treadmills.
9. Do a Tripod Stand for 30 seconds.
10. Do a Handstand in a hula hoop for 10 seconds.

COOPERATIVE FITNESS (1–8)

Focus: Overall fitness, cooperation

Equipment: Beanbags, folding mats, jump ropes, task cards

Description:

Various individual, partner, and small group activities designed for maximum motivation and development of overall fitness. Specific components of fitness and motor-skill development are addressed by each challenge.

Procedure:

Each activity is designed to challenge students at various skill and fitness levels. Give instruction to insure proper technique is used. Arrange stations with various task cards around the facility. Assign students to stations for a period at a time and challenge them to "master" a predetermined number of activities.

Muscular Strength and Endurance:

1. ***Push-Up/Curl-Up:*** One partner assumes a curl-up position with knees bent, feet flat. The other partner assumes a push-up position with hands on the partner's feet. As one partner curls up, the other does a push-up.

   • How many can you do in 2 minutes? (Switch positions after 1 minute.)

2. ***Partner Spring:*** Partners stand facing each other approximately 2 feet apart. Keeping feet in one place, lean forward, touching hands and simultaneously pushing back.

   • How many springs can you do in 2 minutes without moving your feet?

3. ***Two-Way Push-Up:*** One partner assumes a position on all fours (back flat, weight equally distributed on hands and knees). The other partner, with hands to one side, places both feet on the flat portion of the partner's back. When both are ready, the bottom partner lifts his or her knees off the ground and assumes a push-up position.

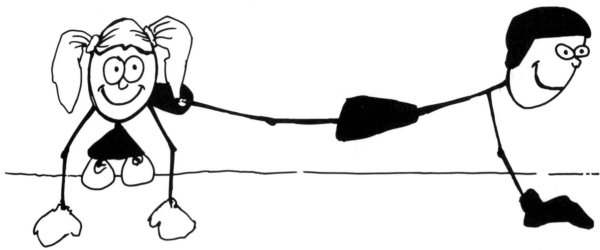

• How many can you do?

4. ***Arm-Over Push-Up:*** Partners assume a push-up position, side by side, facing the same direction. When ready, they place their inside arms over each other's back and do push-ups.

• How many can you do?

5. ***Push-Up Tag:*** Partners assume a push-up position facing each other approximately 6 inches apart. When ready, each person tries to tag the partner's hand as many times as possible in the time limit. **(Caution students not to pull on the arm or tag above the hand.)**

• How many times can you tag your partner's hand?

6. ***Partner Stand:*** Partners stand facing each other, toes touching. They join hands and sit down. Without letting go or moving their feet, they try to stand back up.

- How many times can you stand up and sit down in 1 minute?

7. ***Partner V-Press:*** Partners of similar size sit facing each other with their feet approximately even with the hips of their partner. One partner holds the heels of the other and then lifts the legs above his or her head.

- How many presses can you do in 1 minute?

8. *Lift Off:* Partners sit facing each other with the soles of their feet touching, hands in a rear support position. When ready, both push with their feet and arms and attempt to raise off the ground.

   • Can you lift off? How long can you stay up?

9. *Frisky Pony:* Place the hands on the ground directly in line with the shoulders, like preparing to perform a handstand. Lift the legs off the ground and kick them back before landing back on the ground. *Modification:* Have advanced students bring the hands off the ground when the feet are kicked back and land on the floor in a standing position.

   • How many Frisky Ponies can you do in 2 minutes?

Abdominal Strength:

1. *Basic Partner Curl-Ups:* Partners, facing each other, assume a curl-up position, knees bent, with their feet interlocked. When ready, they sit up and down simultaneously.

   • How many can you do in 2 minutes?

2. *Row Your Boat:* Partners sit facing each other holding hands, soles of their feet touching. Adjust the distance between partners so that each person's legs are slightly bent and each person can almost lie down on his or her back while the other person is in a sitting position. Row back and forth.

   • Can you row continuously for 2 minutes?

3. ***Foot Pass:*** With a partner or in small groups, sit an arm's distance from the next person. One person places a beanbag between his or her feet and passes it to the next person, who takes it with his or her feet. The beanbag is passed around the group or between partners. When a person does not have the beanbag, he or she should be doing curl-ups or rowing.

   • How many complete rotations can the group make in 2 minutes?

4. ***Hand Pass:*** Partners sit facing each other, legs extended. One person holds a beanbag. Both partners raise their legs off the ground 6 to 12 inches with knees slightly bent. They maintain that position and toss the beanbag back and forth. *Modification:* Try this activity in groups of 6 to 8 and pass the beanbag around the group. Those not passing the bag should do curl-ups or rowing.

   • How many passes can you make in 1 minute?

5. ***Bicycle Race:*** Partners sit facing each other with the soles of their feet touching, arms in a rear support position, keeping a comfortable distance apart so that the legs can almost be fully extended. Lift the legs in the air and pretend to be riding a bicycle.

   • Can you "ride" continuously for 2 minutes?

Cardiovascular Endurance:

1. ***Partner Jumping Jacks:*** Holding hands with a partner, try various forms of jumping jacks. The hands can never separate.

   • How many partner jumping jacks can you do in 2 minutes? How many variations can you do?

2. ***Partner Locomotor Challenges:*** With partners linked together, perform various locomotor movements around the perimeter of the facility. Some ways to link together are: (1) holding hands, (2) back to back, (3) elbows interlocked, (4) facing each other with hands on each other's shoulders. Examples of locomotor activities include: (1) sliding, (2) grapevine step, (3) skipping, (4) backwards walking, (5) hopping, (6) leaping.

   • How many different linkages and movements can you do in 2 minutes?

3. ***Shadows:*** This activity requires a teacher/leader and an open space. On the

start signal, one partner begins running anywhere in the designated area. The partner tries to stay as close as possible without touching or running into the other. The runner may go in any direction, change directions, or reverse directions. On the stop signal, both partners must stop. The "following" partner may take one step toward the "leader" and try to reach him or her. If he or she does, score a point. Reverse roles and begin again.

- How many points can you score in 2 minutes?

4. ***Shoulder Tag:*** Partners face each other an arm's distance apart. Each person moves in a small designated area trying to touch the partner's shoulder. Each person keeps track of the number of touches made. ***Safety:*** **Make certain there is enough distance between groups so too much contact does not take place.**

5. ***Inside/Outside Relay:*** This activity is for the entire class. Partners, standing side by side and facing the same direction, are spread around the perimeter of the facility. On the start signal, the inside person begins briskly walking the perimeter; at the same time, the outside partner begins jogging the perimeter. When the outside person reaches the inside partner, they switch places and continue the pattern.

- How many times can you switch places in 2 minutes?

6. ***Jog and Touch:*** This activity is for the entire class. Partners are spread out around the perimeter of the facility. They join hands and, on the start signal, begin jogging and touching as many groups as possible within the designated time period.

- How many groups can you touch in 1 minute?

7. ***Line Touch:*** This activity is for the entire class. Partners spread out around the facility holding hands. On the start signal, they begin jogging and touching as many lines with their hands as possible within the designated time period. *Modification:* (1) Start at one end of the facility and have the students run to the other end, touch the line, and return. (2) Have the students assume different "holding" positions; e.g., arms around waist, shoulders, etc. (3) Perform as a group of 6 to 8 students.

- How many lines can you touch in 1 minute?

8. ***Fast Pass:*** This activity is for the entire class. Divide the class into two groups, each standing on opposite sides of the facility. On the start signal, call out a designated locomotor movement. Students then quickly move to the other side of the area using that movement. They must not bump into anyone else. Upon reaching the opposite side, they jump in the air and turn 180 degrees, clap their hands, and sit down. When all students have completed the task, repeat using a different movement. *Modification:* (1) If a student bumps into another person, they both must stop and raise their hands, creating an obstacle for others to move around. After the others have reached the sides, they may go. (2) Decrease the area width each time until the group must co-

operate to get across without bumping. (3) Increase the pace. As soon as students reach one side and are sitting, give the start signal.

- How many successful passes can you make?

9. ***High Fives:*** This activity is for the entire class. Have the students move throughout the facility performing a designated locomotor movement. Each time they pass another person, give that person a "jumping" high five. *Modification and safety:* (1) Have the students give "low" high fives or "regular" high fives. (2) Caution the students not to slap hands.

- How many high fives can you give in 2 minutes?

10. ***Jump and Touch:*** Have partners face each other. Both partners jump as high in the air as possible. At the "top" of their jump, they raise their arms as high as possible and lightly touch fingertips. *Hint:* If students are not matched by height, one partner must angle his or her hands downward to make the touch.

- How many touches can you make in 1 minute?

11. ***Speed Skipping:*** Students are arranged in pairs with one jump rope per group. One person assumes the role of "speed skipper" while the other one is the "counter." The counter gives the start signal and the skipper begins jumping as fast as possible using a jogging step. The counter counts the number of times the skipper's right foot touches the ground during the designated time period. No deduction is made for misses. At the end of the time period, the partners switch roles.

- How many steps can you do in 2 minutes?

THE PASSING JOGGER (2-5)

Focus: Cardiovascular endurance, hand-eye coordination

Equipment: Beanbag, balls

Description:

A challenging activity that combines various locomotor activities with tossing and catching skills. Although the basic activity appears to be simple, increased difficulty and greater challenges are presented through the modifications.

Procedure:

Begin with students in a large circle standing a minimum of 5 feet apart. Give each person a beanbag (or a ball for more advanced groups).

1. On the start signal, students begin walking, or slowly jogging, in a clockwise direction. Make sure they maintain their spacing.
2. Once a pace is established, have students toss their object in the air and catch it.
3. On the stop signal, have students "freeze" and toss their object over their head to the person behind them.
4. When each student has an object, begin moving again.

Modifications:

The activity above is the basic activity. If students are having trouble with this activity, review tossing and catching skills before continuing.

1. Have students jog or perform other locomotor activities while tossing.
2. Have several circles or make patterns allowing groups to cross, etc.
3. Give a "reverse" signal and have students change directions.
4. Specify different types of tosses and catches; e.g., one hand toss/catch toss with one hand; catch with another; toss, clap, and catch.
5. Change objects. Use small balls, Frisbees™, etc., to increase difficulty.
6. Have students in a scattered formation and, on signal, have them change directions; e.g., move to their left, move to their right.
7. Arrange students in groups, each with a leader who determines the direction to move.
8. Give every third student an object and, on signal, they toss it over their head to the person behind them.
9. Have all students with an object, on signal, toss it to the person behind. This involves cooperation and listening skills, good initial class organization, and offers a challenge.

AEROBIC INTERVAL WARM-UP (2–8)

Focus: Prepare for more strenuous activity, flexibility

Equipment: Tape player, music

Description:

A quick warm-up activity designed to prepare students for a more vigorous, high energy activity.

Procedure:

Have students move to an open space that gives them enough space to move without bumping others. Use the following routine. Have students perform each activity for approximately 30 to 45 seconds, depending on the age and activity level.

Sample Routine:

Simulate rope skipping without ropes for 30 seconds between each exercise activity. Use varied steps and assure that the arms are moving appropriately.

Trunk Twister	Front Straddle Stretch
Bend and Reach	Inner Thigh Stretch
Side Flex	Starter Stretch
Down/Up Swing	Jogging in place while performing arm lifts

ENDLESS MILE (2-8)

Focus: Cardiovascular

Equipment: Football flag or beanbag

Description:

A cooperative fitness activity designed to assist students in refining pacing skills as well as developing cardiovascular fitness.

Procedure:

Arrange students in a single-file line approximately 5 feet apart around the perimeter of the facility. The first person in line is given a football flag or beanbag.

1. When the start signal is given, students begin a slow jog around the perimeter.
2. After completing one lap, the first person raises the "signal" and the last person in the line begins sprinting on the outside of the line until he or she assumes the lead.
3. Upon assuming the lead, that person returns to a slow jog and raises the "signal" for the last person to begin his or her sprint.
4. Continue this process until all students have returned to their starting positions.

Modifications:

1. When the "sprinter" is approximately two-thirds of the way to the front, have the front person raise the signal for the next person to begin sprinting.
2. Divide the class into two groups, one performing the "Endless Mile" and the other performing "Basic Teacher/Leader Exercises" in the center of the facility. With this modification, students can be arranged according to cardiovascular fitness levels.
3. Speed up the pattern of the last person sprinting by blowing a whistle every 30 seconds, indicating the next person in line is to begin his or her sprint.

FITNESS OBSTACLE COURSE (2-8)

Focus: Overall fitness, coordination, motor-skill development

Equipment: As needed per stations, directional cards or markers

Description:

An obstacle fitness course that provides traditional and nontraditional activities to physically challenge students.

Procedure:

Set up stations approximately 15 to 20 feet apart throughout the facility. Have directional cards or markers that indicate the next obstacle to which the students are to proceed. Divide the class into two groups. One group performs the obstacle course while the other group works on alternative activities; e.g., juggling, double dutch.

1. Have the group that is working on the obstacle course lined up behind the first station.
2. On the start signal, the first person moves to the first station. When he or she is halfway to the second station, the next student begins.
3. Rotate groups after each student has gone through the course two times.

Efficiency and Challenges:

1. Demonstrate the course before having students begin.
2. Determine stations depending on the ability of the class. All skills should have already been introduced in one form or another so that all students may be successful.
3. Designate one locomotor movement between obstacles. You can designate one movement for the entire course or change after each obstacle. Task cards should be made to designate locomotor movement if it is to be changed.

Sample Obstacle Courses

Beginning Level: Start ----> hurdle over 3 wands ----> crawl under folded mat ----> crab walk 10 feet

Finish <- - - - |

Figure 8
run around
cones
∧
⋮
'----- jump 10 feet <---- through hoops <---- run around cones
       rabbit   hop scotch   figure 8

Intermediate Level:

Start ----> jump over 6 wands ----> jump through hoops ----> crab walk 15 feet

Finish <- - - -

hurdle 2 cones
∧
⋮
climb ropes   hop scotch   forward   figure 8
to 12' <---- through hoops <---- roll length <----rabbit jump
                                   of 2 mats

Advanced Level:

Start ----> bear walk ----> crawl through 2 mats ----> jump through hoops ----> crab walk 15 feet *or Bridge walk*
(laying on stomach)

        Finish   Hurdle 4 cones
∧
crab walk
15 feet
∧
⋮
run through   hop scotch   leg extension   rabbit jump   jump over
hoops   <---- through hoops <---- climbing ropes <---- through cones <---- 6 wands
                                  6 times

FITNESS RELAY (2-8)

Focus: Cardiovascular endurance, coordination

Equipment: Cones, task cards

Description:

A relay-type activity encompassing various fitness and locomotor activities in a challenging format.

Procedure:

Set cones in lines of four approximately 15 feet apart for beginners; 20 feet for intermediates; and 25 feet for advanced students. There should be one set of cones for each group of 6 to 7 students. Place on each cone a task card indicating the activity to be done at that cone and the locomotor movement to be used to get to the next cone. Divide the class into groups of 6 to 7 and assign each group to a line of cones.

1. On the start signal, the first student in each group performs the locomotor movement on the first task card to the next cone.
2. Upon arriving at cone 2, they perform the activity listed and move to cone 3.
3. Upon reaching cone 4 and prior to beginning the activity, the student calls out "BULLDOG" (or whatever your mascot is) and then performs the listed activity.
4. Upon hearing "BULLDOG" the next student in line begins to move to cone 2.
5. After completing the activity at cone 4, the students perform an Animal Walk (no Elephant Walks) back to the line.
6. Continue until all students have gone through twice.

Modifications:

1. Have two students go at the same time from each line.
2. Have students waiting for a turn jog in place or simulate rope jumping.

Organization:

For this activity a specific number of repetitions to complete at each station should be listed instead of a time. As the instructor you will need to move in and out of the groups to make certain they are performing the correct number of repetitions.

Sample Relay Activities:

LOCOMOTOR MOVEMENTS	CONE ACTIVITIES
Two-foot jump	cone 1: modified Push-Up
Skipping	cone 2: modified Curl-Up
Galloping	cone 3: Kick Through
One-foot hop	cone 4: Treadmill

ANIMAL WALK BACK TO LINE

74

GROUP AND LEADER EXERCISES (2-8)

Focus: Overall fitness, leadership skills

Equipment: Task cards, jump ropes, etc.

Description:

This is a modified approach to the "Basic Teacher/Leader Exercises" described earlier. Students are arranged in individual groups of 5 to 7 students each, with a student leader who takes the groups through a series of exercise/activities.

Procedure:

Assign students to groups of 5 to 7 each. A leader is assigned or chosen by the group. Give each group a task card with a series of exercise/activities listed. Provide necessary equipment for each group and assign each to an area of the facility.

1. On the start signal, each group begins its exercise/activities.
2. Move around to the groups, assisting where necessary and offering encouragement.

Hints and Modification:

1. Have a different task card for each group so that on successive days, groups will participate in different activities.
2. Change leaders for each activity within a group, thus creating a greater opportunity for leadership each day.
3. Perform this activity for several days so that all students have a chance to lead.

Suggested Time Frames for Groups:

Beginner: Perform the exercises for 30 seconds and end with a 2-minute jog.

Intermediate: Perform the exercises for 40 seconds each and end with 3 minutes of rope skipping.

Advanced: Perform the exercises for 60 seconds each and end with a 5-minute jog.

Sample Exercises:

These activities represent a sample of those that can be used. *Be creative* and make up your own.

Beginner: Select 1 activity from each group.

Intermediate: Select 2 activities from each group.

Advanced: Select 2 activities from each group.

GROUP 1	**GROUP 2**	**GROUP 3**	**GROUP 4**
Curl-Up	Push-Up	Treadmill	Sit and Reach
Rowing	Crab Walk	Squat Thrust	Windmill
V-Up	Animal Walk	Ski Jump	Sitting Toe Touch
Leg Extension	Pull-Up	Side Flex	Heel Slap

ROPE-SKIPPING FOR FITNESS (2–8)

Focus: Cardiovascular endurance, muscular endurance

Equipment: Jump rope

Description:

Various rope-skipping patterns designed to motivate and challenge students of all ability levels as well as to increase overall fitness levels.

Procedure:

Have students select the proper length rope; i.e., the student should stand with feet together on the center of the rope. Lifting the rope up by each handle, the handles should extend to the armpit when pulled tight. The rope may be from 1 to 2 inches shorter, but no longer. After selecting a rope, students select a partner and move to an open space. Have them warm up by jumping slowly for 2 minutes; this is a good time to have them try various steps and stunts to provide more challenge and motivation.

1. Begin the fitness set by having one person jump for a specified time while the partner times the activity and keeps track of the number of jumps in that time period.
2. The partners switch after the specified time period.
3. At the conclusion of the fitness set(s), all students should cool-down by jumping slowly for 2 minutes.

Organization:

Rope-skipping is a near perfect exercise that utilizes both the upper and lower body to improve overall fitness levels and coordination skills. In order for students to gain the maximum benefits possible, each student must be challenged—but not frustrated—by being asked to perform steps or skills above their developmental level. It is suggested that basic jogging steps and two-foot jumps be used for the development of fitness. Students should be challenged to improve their rope-skipping skills during the warm-up portion of the set and during instructional periods related to rope-skipping.

Definitions of Fitness-Related Rope-Skipping Terms:

1. *Speed Play:* A combination of slow, medium, and fast rope-skipping speeds for a predetermined period of time. The student should determine when to speed up, to what level of speed, how long to hold the speed, when to slow down, and how long before the next speed period, etc. Incorporate a variety of steps for fun.
2. *Surges:* Sprints (short speed-skipping periods) are spaced into a long endurance period. Hold the speed surge for 1 to 3 minutes, depending on condition and length of the endurance period, before dropping back to base speed. Repeat 2 to 6 times in an endurance period.

3. ***Long and Fast:*** Turn the rope at near maximum speed as can be held for the predetermined length of time (2 to 3 minutes).

4. ***Intervals:*** The intervals between each maximum speed period is controlled in length and activity. Either rest or skip rope easily during each measured interval. Build up over a period of weeks by going faster between intervals or by going longer between intervals.

5. ***Pyramids:*** Begin with a slow base rope speed. Increase the rope speed by 6 to 8 turns of the rope per minute and hold for 1 to 2 minutes. Increase the speed again by 6 to 8 turns per minute and hold 1 to 2 minutes. Repeat until maximum rope speed is achieved, then drop by the same increments of speed and time until base speed is attained. Repeat 1 to 4 sets, depending on individual student fitness levels.

6. ***Half Pyramids:*** Build in increments from base rope speed as in Pyramids above. After maximum rope speed has been maintained for the desired period of time, drop immediately back to the beginning base rope speed. (Repeat 1 to 6 sets.)

7. ***Repeats:*** Turn the rope at maximum speed for a specified length of time (1 to 5 minutes). Recover by resting or slow rope-skipping until the heart rate drops to below student's target rate, then repeat the exercise. (Repeat 2 to 8 times.)

8. ***Doubles:*** Do continuous double-unders for 20 to 30 seconds. Rest for 30 seconds and repeat the bout. (Repeat 2 to 12 times.)

Sample Fitness Progression:

Amount listed in turns per minute (tpm), 30-second rest between sets. (Adapted from material developed by Paul Smith of Seattle, WA.)

WEEK	BEGINNER	INTERMEDIATE	ADVANCED
1	100 tpm for 1 minute, 3 sets	110 tpm for 1 minute, 2 sets	120 tpm for 1 minute, 2 sets
2	100 tpm for $1\frac{1}{2}$ minutes	110 tpm for $1\frac{1}{2}$ minutes, 2 sets	speed play for 1 minute, 2 sets
		120 tpm for $1\frac{1}{2}$ minutes, 1 set	120 tpm for 2 minutes, 1 set
3	110 tpm for 2 minutes	110 tpm for 2 minutes, 3 sets	Interval, 3 sets
4	110 tpm for 2 minutes	110 tpm for 2 minutes, 4 sets	Interval, 3 sets
		120 tpm for $1\frac{1}{2}$ minutes, 3 sets	Long and fast, 2 minutes
5	120 tpm for 2 minutes	120 tpm for 2 minutes, 4 sets	Half pyramids, 4 minutes
	100 tpm for 2 minutes	110 tpm for 2 minutes, 2 sets	Pyramids, 1 set
6	120 tpm for $2\frac{1}{2}$ minutes, 1 set	120 tpm for 3 minutes, 2 sets	Interval, 2 sets

RUN FOR FUN (2–8)

Focus: Cardiovascular fitness

Equipment: Jump ropes, task cards

Description:

A less intense variation of "Melt Down." This activity involves performing specific exercise/activities and jogging a predetermined number of laps at the conclusion of each exercise/activity.

Procedure:

Divide the facility into four stations; e.g., one on each side and one on each end. Assign a specific exercise/activity to each station. Divide the class into four equal groups and assign each to a station.

1. On the start signal, students begin performing the exercise/activity for their station for a specified time period.
2. When the time period is completed, students begin to jog the perimeter of the area for a designated number of laps.
3. After jogging, each group rotates clockwise one station and begins to perform the exercise activity.
4. Continue until all stations have been completed and cool-down with jogging 2 laps and walking 1 lap.

Sample Activities and Times:

LEVEL	LAPS TO RUN	EXERCISE TIME
Beginner	2	60 seconds
Intermediate	3	90 seconds
Advanced	3	120 seconds

Activities for Each Station:

1. *Hop-Line Push-Ups:* Students assume a push-up position with hands placed over a line. To begin, students punch up with the arms, lifting the hands off the ground and landing on the other side of the line. This motion is continued for the duration of the exercise. *Note:* This is an advanced push-up; modifications include walking the hands over the line and doing the push-up from the knees.
2. *Speed Shuttle:* Students stand on a line facing another line approximately 30 feet away. On signal, they run to the line, touch it with their hand, turn, and run back to the starting line. This is repeated until the time is up. Have

students keep track of the number of lines touched. Ask for the number when they are doing the cool-down. Record the number and use it as a motivator.

3. ***Rope-Skipping:*** Students begin rope-skipping for the duration of the time period. Add variations or challenges to enhance motivation.

4. ***Curl-Ups:*** Students begin continuous curl-ups or modified curl-ups for the duration of the time period. *Variation:* Have the students get a partner and sit in a facing position with one person holding a beanbag. Students perform curl-ups and toss the beanbag back and forth during the "up motion."

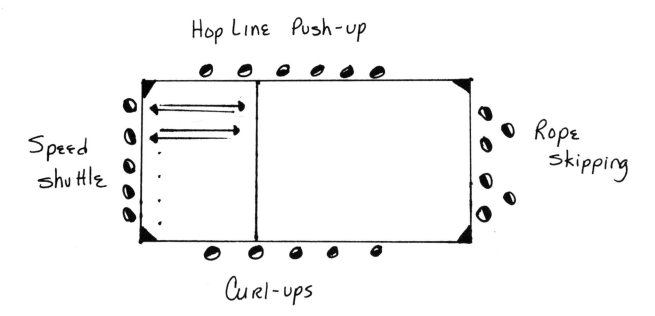

ALTERNATE AEROBICS (3-8)

Focus: Cardiovascular, muscular strength/endurance

Equipment: Tape player, music, jump ropes

Description:

An activity combining aerobics and traditional fitness activities designed to provide motivation along with aerobic and strength training.

Procedure:

Divide students into two groups, forming two circles one inside the other. The inside circle faces the outside circle.

1. Begin both groups with an aerobic routine lasting for approximately 3 minutes.
2. At the conclusion of the aerobic set, the outside group begins an exercise set while the inside group continues with an aerobic activity.
3. After the designated time, the groups switch activities and begin again.
4. Continue alternating until the activity is completed.
5. Conclude with a 1-minute aerobic set for all students, followed by a 2-minute cool-down.

Sample Activities:

The times in the following examples are designed for one group; therefore, the time for the entire activity would be double. The aerobic activity could be jumping rope, continuing jogging in a circle, mountain climbers, or a set aerobic routine.

BEGINNER:

Aerobic set	3 minutes
Push-Ups (variations)	30 seconds
Aerobics	30 seconds
Curl-Ups	30 seconds
Aerobics	30 seconds
Chair/Bench Dips	30 seconds
Aerobics	30 seconds
Crab Kicks	30 seconds
Aerobics	1 minute
Cool-Down/Walk	2 minutes

INTERMEDIATE:

Repeat the beginner level, but only do the last aerobic and cool-down once.

ADVANCED:

Perform the beginner level two times and increase time to 40 seconds.

AUTOBAHN* (3-8)

Focus: Cardiovascular, muscular strength/endurance, cooperation skills

Equipment: Plastic bats, jump ropes, cones

Description:

A cooperative aerobic relay that involves students working as partners and individuals to complete the assigned activities.

Procedure:

Place one cone for each team in the center of the facility. In front of each cone, place one plastic bat and two jump ropes. Divide students into traditional line-relay formation with four students per line.

1. Have each group of four stand behind a cone in the center of the facility facing, in one direction, the sideline.
2. On the "start" command, the first two students each take one end of their group's bat and begin jogging the perimeter of the facility holding the bat between them.
3. The remaining students in each line get a jump rope and beginning jumping in place.
4. This continues until the "joggers" have completed two laps. When they return to their line after the two laps, the team members switch activities.
5. Continue until all team members have jogged six laps.

Modifications and Challenges:

This activity is a lead-up to an "Autobahn Challenge" and should be introduced one day prior to moving into the modification/challenge listed below.

1. Once the students are doing their aerobic activity, every 10 to 15 seconds call out one of the commands listed below.
2. When given a command, all students immediately stop the aerobic activity and perform the activity associated with the command.
3. After they have successfully performed the activity for the specified time, the command "green light" is given and all students resume the aerobic activity.

---

*This activity has been modified from "Speedway," presented at the Washington State Elementary Tour '88 workshop by Jerry Poppen, Tacoma School District, Tacoma, WA.

4. For an additional challenge, have both partners maintain continuous contact with the plastic bat while doing the selected activity.

SAMPLE COMMAND	TASK	TIME PERFORMED (beginner—intermediate—advanced)
Flat Tire	Push-Ups	15—20—25 seconds
Spin Out	Sitting Spins	15—20—25 seconds
Overheated	Crab Kicks	15—20—25 seconds
Oil Leak	Mountain Climbers	15—20—25 seconds
Out of Gas	Jumping Jacks	15—20—25 seconds
Red Light	Curl-Ups	15—20—25 seconds
Yellow Light	Jump and Touch	15—20—25 seconds
Green Light	Resume Activity	

AUTOBAHN

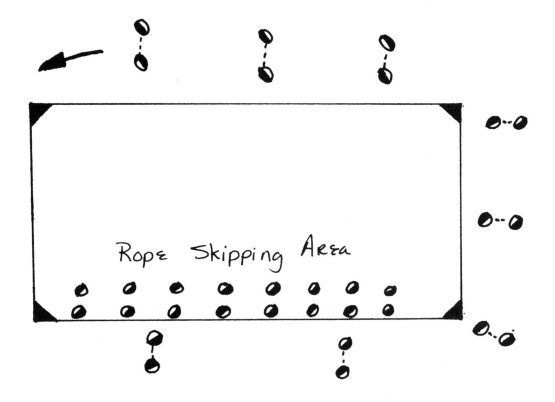

Rope Skipping Area

BASIC CIRCUIT EXERCISES (3-8)

Focus: Enhancement of overall fitness

Equipment: Stations, cones, task cards

Description:

A series of predetermined stations utilizing a group of exercises/activities conducted for specific time periods. Groups of students rotate to each station in the circuit until all stations are completed.

Procedure:

Set up various stations around the facility with enough space for 4 to 6 students to participate at one time. Place task cards on cones or on the wall near each station describing what activity is to be done. Divide students into groups according to the number of stations set up; e.g., 6 stations = 6 groups.

1. Give the "go" signal for students to begin exercising.
2. When the predetermined time for activity has been achieved, give the signal to rotate.
3. Students rotate in a clockwise manner one station. Give 10 to 15 seconds for the rotation before signaling students to begin the activity.
4. Continue until all groups have completed all stations.
5. Conclude with a 2-minute slow jog and a 1-minute cool-down walk.

Organization:

1. A fixed time period at each station offers the best organization for this activity. For example:

Beginner	30 to 35 seconds per station
Intermediate	45 to 60 seconds per station
Advanced	60 to 90 seconds per station

2. Each station should focus on a different fitness component; i.e., abdominal, upper body, lower body, fitness, cardiovascular. In the case of advanced circuits, place activities that work the same fitness component next to each other in the rotation, thus providing a more strenuous workout.

Sample Routine Circuit

Beginning Level (6 station)

Arm Circles	Half Curl-Ups	Side Flex
Rowing	Crab Walk	Rope Skipping

Intermediate Level (8 station)

Push-ups	Curl-ups	Treadmill
Jogging in Place		Rope Skipping
Squat Thrust	Leg Extensions	Crab Walk

Advanced Level (10 station)

Reclining Pull-ups	Curl-ups	Treadmill	Rope Skipping
	Rowing		Push-ups
Spider Push-ups	Rope Skipping	Squat Thrust	Leg Extensions

IT'S IN THE CARDS* (3-8)

Focus: Cardiovascular, muscular strength/endurance, coordination

Equipment: Task sheets, cards, jump ropes, balls, beanbags, mats

Description:

An activity that provides a unique approach to improving fitness through the use of cards and cooperation. Students perform activities both individually and as a group depending on the cards they are dealt.

Procedure:

Stations are arranged throughout the facility to accommodate teams of five students each. At each station place one task sheet; one deck of cards; three each of jump ropes, beanbags, and playground balls; and one mat. Assign each group of five to a station. Designate one student to be the dealer in each group.

1. On the signal the dealer deals one card (face down) to each team member, including himself or herself.
2. After each person has a card, the dealer calls "over."
3. Each person looks at his or her card and performs the corresponding activity listed on the task sheet.
4. When the last member of the group completes his or her task, the used cards are placed in the center, face up, and the dealer deals a new hand.
5. Repeat this process until each group has gone through its deck.

Modification:

When first introducing this activity to beginners, use one set of cards for the entire class. Have the dealer take one card from the deck and return to his or her group. All students in that group perform the same activity.

Sample Tasks:

ACE:	Takes precedence over all cards. If one person in the group gets an ACE, the entire group runs 1 lap.
KING:	Perform 10 Push-Ups. (Use individual variations.)
QUEEN:	Toss-turn-catch a ball 5 times.
JACK:	Perform 25 Jumping Jacks.

*This is a modification of an activity shared by Chuck Ayers of the Bellingham School District at the 1987 WAHPERD Conference and as published by L. F. Turner in *A Teacher's Skill by Skill Guide for Physical Education* (Parker Publishing Company, West Nyack, NY, 1990).

JOKER: Perform 5 Figure-Eight Passes with a ball.

HEARTS: Perform that specific number of Jump-Rope turns.

SPADES: Perform that number of Curl-Ups. (Individual variations.)

DIAMONDS: Perform that number of Bench Dips.

CLUBS: Perform that number of modified Handstands or perform a Handstand for that number of seconds.

3/KIND: Free pass for the entire group. Deal new cards.

FITNESS CENTER (3-8)

Focus: Cardiovascular endurance, muscular strength, flexibility

Equipment: Spinner, task cards, jump ropes, benches, balls, hand weight

Description:

A nontraditional fitness circuit utilizing a spinner to direct students to exercise stations, and task cards at each station directing them to specific activities.

Procedure:

Arrange "fitness clubs" in each quadrant of the facility. Each "fitness club" has specific activities to be completed placed on a task card taped to the wall or on a cone and the appropriate equipment. Arrange students in a line around the perimeter and place the "spinner" in the center.

1. On the start signal, all students begin a slow jog around the facility.
2. After approximately 2 laps, the spinner is spun and all students stop jogging.
3. When the spinner stops, individuals in that color club (quadrant) continue jogging. The rest of the students go to the club color they are in and begin to perform the tasks listed; e.g., if the spinner stops on red, the red students continue to jog and all other students go and begin their activity.
4. Each group should perform the activities in the clubs for 1 to 3 minutes, beginner–advanced respectively.
5. After the designated time, all students begin jogging until the next spin.
6. Allow a minimum of 30 seconds of jogging before spinning.

Spinner Construction:

Take a 4 × 4 piece of cardboard and divide it into four equal parts. Mark each section with a color. Punch a hole in the center and attach a binder clip to serve as a spinner. You can also use different game spinners and modify the game board to fit this activity.

Club Cards:

RED CLUB (Cardiovascular)

Treadmill
Jump Rope (variations)
Hoop Hopping
Jumping Jacks (variations)

BLUE CLUB (Abdominal)

Crunches
Curl-Ups
Continuous Rowing
Ball Catch Sit-Ups

YELLOW CLUB (Upper Body)

Hop-Line Push-Ups
Bench Dips
Overhead Press with Hand Weights

GREEN CLUB (Flexibility)

V-Sit and Reach
Body Bender
Sit and Reach

Facility Set-Up:

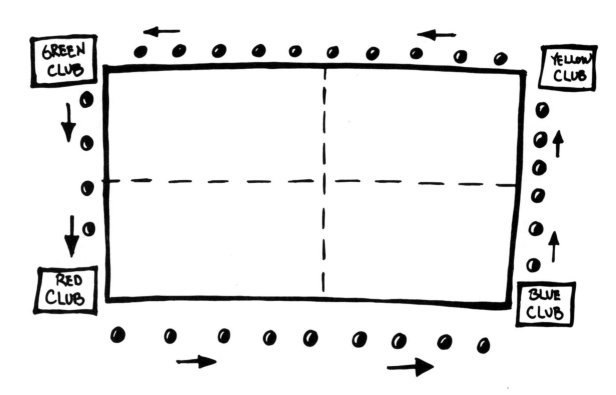

FOUR-CORNER RUN (3-8)

Focus: Cardiovascular endurance, muscular strength

Equipment: Task cards

Description:

A fast-moving activity utilizing small groups in a pattern-running movement coupled with various exercise/activities. Groups can be arranged according to fitness/skill level or in a random manner.

Procedure:

Divide students into equal groups with each group assigned to an area where a 20′ × 20′ square has been marked. At each corner of the square, place task cards listing basic exercise activities.

1. When the "start" signal is given, the first student in each group begins to run the pattern.
2. Upon reaching the first corner, they perform the listed exercise/activity.
3. When the first person reaches the first corner, the second person begins to run.
4. When a corner activity is completed, the student continues with the running pattern until all corner activities have been completed.
5. When all corner activities are completed, the student returns to the end of the line and waits for another turn.
6. Continue until students have had a minimum of 3 turns for beginners, 4 turns for intermediates, and 5 turns for advanced. (Advanced students should conclude with a 3-minute jog.)

Modification:

For a fast-moving aerobic activity, eliminate the corner activities. Have the students record the number of completed "squares" within the specified time period.

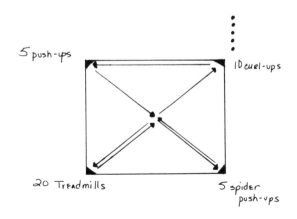

GROUP CIRCUIT (3-8)

Focus: Cardiovascular endurance, muscular strength

Equipment: Task cards, as needed for specific tasks

Description:

A fitness activity that combines aerobics and traditional exercises into an eight-station circuit.

Procedure:

Set up an eight-station circuit around the perimeter of the facility. Have all students move to a scatter formation in the center of the area and count off by 8.

1. Begin the activity with students in the center performing 3 minutes of aerobic activity.
2. After the initial aerobics, the students run to their first station, e.g., number 1's to station 1, etc., and perform the tasks listed for 1 minute.
3. On signal they run back to the center and begin a second aerobic set lasting for 1 minute.
4. After that aerobic set, they move to the station to the left of the one last performed.
5. Continue this alternating pattern until all stations are completed.
6. Conclude with 1 or 2 minutes of walking.

Variation:

Instead of assigning a starting station for students, let them go to the station of their choice. Make sure they complete all stations by the end of the period.

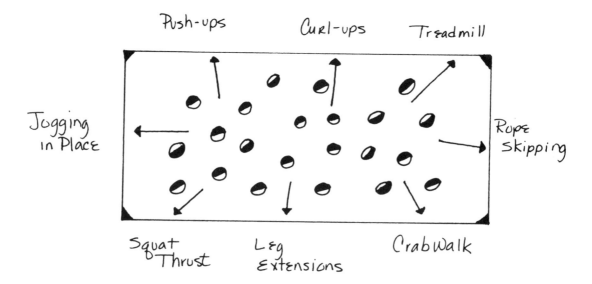

GROUP STATION RUN (3-8)

Focus: Cardiovascular endurance, muscular strength

Equipment: Task cards, as needed for stations

Description:

This activity involves students participating in small groups (determined by individual fitness/skill levels), jogging laps, and performing various exercise/activities as noted on task cards.

Procedure:

Arrange students in groups of 4 to 5 each based on fitness/skill levels. Establish a "home area" for each group and provide an appropriate-level task card for that group.

1. On the start signal, all groups begin jogging for 2 minutes.
2. At the conclusion of the jog, a signal is given and all students/groups return to their "home area" and complete the first exercise/activity listed.
3. After they have completed the activity, they jog 1 lap, return, and complete the second activity.
4. Each group continues until all exercise/activities have been completed and concludes with a 2-lap jog and 1-lap walk.

Modification:

Instead of grouping students based on ability, have them find their own groups of 4 to 5 members. Since the groups are not ability-based, each group would be given the same task card. You can also use the task cards as provided with "Fitness Task Cards."

Sample Task Cards:

TASK CARD
LEVEL 1

1. Do 15 Knee Push-Ups.
2. Do 5 Curl-Ups.
3. Do 20 Treadmills.
4. Jump Rope for 1 minute.
5. Sit and Reach.

TASK CARD
LEVEL 2

1. Do 10 Push-Ups.
2. Do 10 Curl-Ups.
3. Do 50 Treadmills.
4. Jump Rope for 1 minute.
5. Sit and Reach.

TASK CARD
LEVEL 3

1. Do 15 Push-Ups.
2. Do 20 Curl-Ups.
3. Jump Rope for 2 minutes.
4. Do 20 Kick-Throughs.
5. Sit and Reach.

TASK CARD
LEVEL 4

1. Do 12 Chair Dips.
2. Do 15 Crunches.
3. Jump Rope for 2 minutes.
4. Do 30 Kick-Throughs.
5. Sit and Reach.

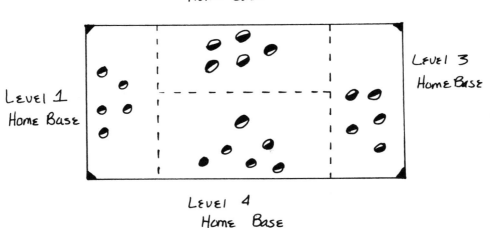

INSIDE-OUTSIDE ROTATION (3-8)

Focus: Cardiovascular endurance, muscular strength

Equipment: Jump ropes, cones or markers

Description:

A nontraditional fitness activity involving running and various strength activities combined in a motivational and challenging format.

Procedure:

Have students pair with a partner. Try using a variety of grouping methods; e.g., random jogging, stop on signal toe to toe with a partner (give 5 seconds). After partners have been selected, have them spread out around the perimeter of the facility and stand back to back—one facing in and one out. Keep groups about 7 to 10 feet apart.

1. On the start signal, the person on the OUTSIDE begins to jog clockwise around the perimeter while the inside partner begins to perform the designated exercise/activity until his or her partner returns.

2. When partners have returned to their original places, the inside group begins to jog while the outside group performs the exercise/activity.

3. Continue until all students have completed each exercise/activity. Conclude with all students jogging for 2 minutes (inside group jogs clockwise—outside group jogs counterclockwise).

Sample Exercises:

Rope-Skipping	Crunches	Curl-Ups
Rowing	Sit and Reach	Push-Ups
V-Ups	Lateral Stretch	Treadmill

Organization:

1. Work with the students who are jogging to run at a fairly slow pace, thus giving appropriate time for the exercise/activities.

2. Have intermediate and advanced students jog 2 laps instead of 1 before switching.

INDIVIDUAL 60-SECOND PREDICTION (3-8)

Focus: Increase overall fitness levels

Equipment: Cones, playground ball, jump ropes, score cards

Description:

A challenging fitness activity presented in a format that allows for improvement of fitness levels and reinforcement of math skills. Students are asked to predict their results in performing various fitness tasks.

Procedure:

Four stations are arranged in the facility. Divide the class into four equal groups, give each person a score card, and assign each group to a station.

1. Based on the particular task, each student writes down a predicted score for the station assigned.
2. On the start command, students begin performing the activity for 60 seconds.
3. When the time is up, they write their actual score, compare it with the predicted score, and move to the next station.
4. Repeat until all stations have been completed.
5. Ask the students to look at their score cards and analyze their predictions and actual scores.

Modifications:

1. Increase the number of stations.
2. Let students work with partners and combine scores.
3. Increase the number of stations and have groups work in a relay fashion, with each group member participating in three or four of the total stations.

Sample Stations:

1. *Jump Rope Variations:*
   - How many consecutive (*insert skill*) can you do in 60 seconds?
2. *Wall Touch:*
   - Facing a wall 30 feet away, how many times can you run, touch the wall, and return in 60 seconds?
3. *Ball Jump:*
   - Placing a ball between your knees, how many times can you jump to a line 15 feet away and back without dropping the ball?

4. *Curl-Ups:*

- With a partner, lie down, bend the knees, and hook ankles together. How many curl-ups can you do in 60 seconds?

Prediction Score Card:

Can You Predict Your Score?

Name: _____ Date: _____

Activity	Prediction	Actual	Total
Consecutive Double-Unders			
Wall Touch			
Ball Jump			
Curl-Up			

INDIVIDUAL TUG-OF-WAR ROPES (3–8)

Focus: Muscular strength

Equipment: One rope for every two students

Description:

Using this simple nontraditional piece of equipment, students perform various partner and small-group strength-building activities. Isometric as well as isotonic activities are performed, which require cooperation with others as well as development of muscular strength.

Procedure:

Pair students with someone of their own strength and ability level. Once paired, each group should take a rope and move to an open space away from walls, obstructions, and others. Caution students not to release their end of the rope in order to prevent injury. In addition, students should let their partner know if his or her grip is slipping so the partner can stop pulling.

1. The following basics should be reviewed:

   a. Pull, don't tug.
   b. For isometrics, pull for approximately 10 to 15 seconds.
   c. If your partner is easily pulled, stop and try again, allowing both partners to work cooperatively for maximum benefit.

2. Instruct students as to the "pull" that will be used and give the start signal.
3. Give the stop signal and have students return to their starting position.
4. Repeat this process for 7 to 10 different pulls, each working on different muscle groups. Or concentrate on one or two groups using various pulls.

Organization and Safety:

1. Work out a system of partner rotation so that each student will have a variety of evenly matched partners.
2. Make sure that students do not do Leg Pulls from a standing position.
3. Do not allow students to pull others around the facility.
4. Continually remind students not to "jerk" or let go.

Sample Activities:

Use various positions to keep interest high and to utilize various muscle groups. The following positions can be used as a reference.
   1. Partners stand facing each other and pulling with:

      a. both hands
      b. right hands

    c. arms above the head

    d. elbows

2. The same as above only from a sitting position.

3. Partners stand back to back, pulling with the same motions as above.

4. Partners on their stomachs, pulling with arms extended in front.

5. Partners sit facing each other, pulling with:

    a. both feet

    b. right foot/left foot

    c. both hands

    d. right hand/left hand

6. Partners grasp the rope with the right/left hand and support the body in a side lead position with the other hand. Both feet on the ground.

7. Partners in a Crab Walk position, trying to pull each other with a hand grip.

8. Instead of having partners pull each other, place a cone 3 to 5 feet behind each person and have them try to knock over the cone.

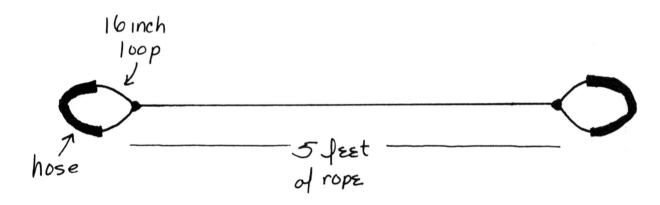

JOGGING TREASURE HUNT (3-8)

Focus: Cardiovascular endurance, muscular strength, motor skills

Equipment: Task cards

Description:

A variation of the "Treasure Hunt" activity using alternating groups of students. As one group is performing activities, the other is jogging.

Procedure:

Divide the class into two groups. One group is stationed in the center of the facility around the task cards. The other group positions itself around the perimeter of the facility.

1. On the start signal, the inside group picks up a task card and begins to perform the listed activity. The outside group then begins to jog the perimeter of the facility.
2. After a predetermined period of time—beginners, 1 minute; intermediates, 2 minutes; advanced, 3 minutes—give the stop signal for the groups to rotate.
3. Continue until all groups have gone through a specified number of rotations.

Organization and Format:

1. The students using the cards may go through two or more cards each rotation depending on the time allowed.
2. Vary the activities to fit the individual levels of each class.

SPEED CIRCUIT (3-8)

Focus: Cardiovascular endurance

Equipment: Jump rope

Description:

A fast-moving aerobic exercise/activity for intermediate- and advanced-level students. Students perform an aerobic activity for a specified period, then do an exercise/activity and return to the aerobic activity as directed.

Procedure:

Have each student get an appropriate length jump rope and move to an open space.

1. On the start signal, students begin the aerobic set by jumping rope.
2. At the end of the designated time period, have students put down the jump rope and immediately move into the exercise/activity.
3. Continue until the entire routine is completed.

Modification:

1. Have the students rest for 2 minutes, then repeat the activity for a more complete aerobic workout lasting the entire class period.
2. Modify the aerobic activity to increase motivation or meet the needs of specific interest groups and individual abilities.
3. Modify the exercise/activities to increase motivation and provide variation and challenge for individual students.

Sample Routine:

Intermediate Level	Activity	Advanced Level
60 seconds	Aerobic	90 seconds
20 seconds	Push-Ups	30 seconds
60 seconds	Aerobic	90 seconds
20 seconds	Rowing	30 seconds
60 seconds	Aerobic	90 seconds
20 seconds	Curl-Ups	90 seconds
60 seconds	Aerobic	90 seconds
30 seconds	Crab Kick	45 seconds
60 seconds	Aerobic	90 seconds
60 seconds	Arm Circles	60 seconds
60 seconds	Aerobic	90 seconds
2 minutes	Walk	2 minutes

SPEED SQUARE (3-8)

Focus: Cardiovascular endurance, muscular strength, coordination skills

Equipment: Cones, task cards

Description:

This simple activity combines locomotor movements with various exercise/activities in a continuous and challenging format. As students move around the perimeter of the facility, they change locomotor movements at predetermined locations and, on signal, stop and perform exercise/activities.

Procedure:

Place cones at each corner of a large square or basketball court, and midway along each side. Attach a task card noting the type of locomotor movement to be used moving from that location to the next. Have students space themselves around the perimeter approximately 6 to 10 feet apart.

1. On the start signal, all students begin moving according to the locomotor movement listed on the card closest to them.
2. At each new card, they change to a new movement.
3. On the stop signal, they stop and perform the exercise/activity called out by the teacher/leader.
4. Once completed they resume their locomotor movements.
5. Continue until all exercise/activities have been completed or for a designated time period.

Organization and Format:

1. Students should be reminded to pass on the outside of slower students while performing their locomotor activities.
2. Exercise/activities should be performed approximately every 30 to 45 seconds.
3. Exercise/activities times are: beginners, 30 seconds; intermediates, 45 seconds; and advanced, 60 seconds.
4. Use music to indicate start and stop; e.g., start locomotor movements when the music starts and stop when the music stops.

Sample Speed-Square Routine:

START (locomotor activity)

STOP—do Curl-Ups (individual variations)

START (locomotor movements)

STOP—do Kick Throughs

START (locomotor movements)

STOP—do Push-Ups (individual variations)
START (locomotor movements)
STOP—do Treadmills
START (locomotor movements)
STOP—do Crab Kicks
START (locomotor activity)
STOP—Bend and Stretch
START (walk slowly for one lap)

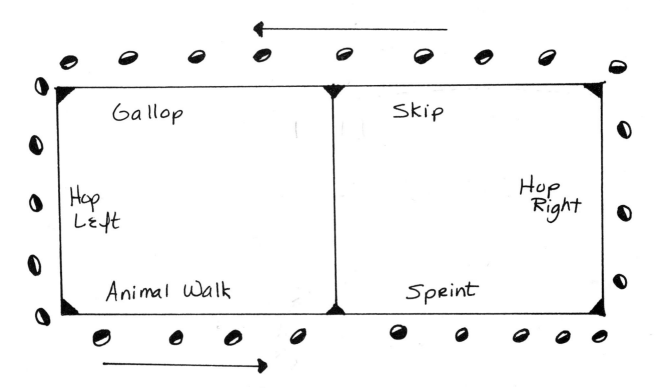

FITNESS TASK CARDS (3-8)

Focus: Cardiovascular endurance, muscular strength

Equipment: Jump ropes, heavy balls, mats, task cards

Description:

Task cards are used to allow the students some freedom while exercising as well as providing variations in the approach to enhancing fitness levels. In addition, they provide you with a written record of student progress related to specific outcomes. The task cards are presented in a sequential progression for students and are activities that have been presented previously. Task cards are divided into four sections, allowing for a complete fitness circuit. The organization of the activities may vary depending on time constraints, facilities, and/or equipment. In some of the activities, the students are to perform for a specified time period and, in others, for a specific number of repetitions.

Procedure:

Divide the class into groups according to the number of stations set up. Within each group have the students get a partner who will time, count, and record. Assign each group to a starting station and let them begin working. Once a student has completed a component, he or she moves to the next until the entire task card has been successfully completed. This may take more than one day. (See the next section.)

Organization and Modification:

1. Have the task cards posted on the wall as well as given to each student.
2. If a student gets "hung up" on one component, let him or her move on. However, students should be given continued assistance in developing the ability to perform the activity.
3. Use the task cards for challenge times during the first or last part of the period. This adds motivation and allows for a variety of activities during the day, thus providing greater opportunities for individual student success.
4. Add a space for student and teacher signatures on each card. Use them as part of your reporting system as examples of student work for their portfolio.

Fitness
Cardiovascular Endurance
TASK CARD 1

Student Check	Teacher Check	CAN YOU?
_____	_____	Jog in place for 1 minute, then quickly walk 2 laps around the facility.
_____	_____	Lay a jump rope in a straight line on the floor and jump over and back 50 times without stopping.
_____	_____	Do a Bunny Jump to a line 20 feet away and jog back. Repeat 4 times without stopping.
_____	_____	Do 50 Treadmills, rest for 15 seconds, and repeat.
_____	_____	Jog the length of the facility and quickly walk the width. Complete 4 laps.

Fitness
Cardiovascular Endurance
TASK CARD 2

Student Check	Teacher Check	CAN YOU?
_____	_____	Jog 5 minutes without stopping, then walk for 2 minutes.
_____	_____	Jump rope at approximately 110 turns per minute for 4 minutes.
_____	_____	Run back and forth 5 times between two lines 30 feet apart in 30 seconds. Rest for 15 seconds and repeat. Repeat 3 times.
_____	_____	Jog 4 laps of the facility, perform a Bunny Jump for $\frac{1}{2}$ lap, and jog 4 more laps.
_____	_____	Jog at a steady pace for 6 minutes and then walk for 2 minutes.

Fitness
Cardiovascular Endurance
TASK CARD 3

Student Check	*Teacher Check*	**CAN YOU?**
_____	_____	Continuously jog for 10 minutes, then walk for 2 minutes.
_____	_____	Do 4 sets of full Jump Rope pyramids, beginning at 110 turns per minute.
_____	_____	Jog 6 laps of the facility, do $\frac{1}{2}$ lap of Bunny Jump, jog 2 laps, do $\frac{1}{2}$ lap of Bunny Jump, jog 1 lap, do $\frac{1}{2}$ lap of Bunny Jump, and walk 1 lap.
_____	_____	Sprint the length of the facility and walk the width. Repeat 10 times.
_____	_____	Jump rope continuously for 10 minutes at approximately 110 turns per minute—"long and slow."

Fitness
Upper Body Strength
TASK CARD 1

Student Check	Teacher Check	**CAN YOU?**
_____	_____	Support yourself in a half Push-Up position for 10 seconds.
_____	_____	Support yourself in a Push-Up position using only your right arm for 30 seconds.
_____	_____	Support yourself in a Push-Up position using only your left arm for 30 seconds.
_____	_____	Perform a feet first Crab Walk for 50 feet without stopping. (Try to keep body as flat as possible while walking. No sagging in the middle!)
_____	_____	Perform a Bar Hang, with chin above bar, for 5 seconds.
_____	_____	Perform 10 modified Push-Ups with good form.
_____	_____	Lying on your back, feet flat, and knees bent, perform 10 Bench Presses using a basketball.

Fitness
Upper Body Strength
TASK CARD 2

Student Check	Teacher Check	CAN YOU?

Student Check *Teacher Check* **CAN YOU?**

_____ _____ Support yourself in a half Push-Up position for 30 seconds.

_____ _____ Support yourself in a Push-Up position and pass a beanbag back and forth with a partner who is 2 feet away. Do 5 times each without missing.

_____ _____ Perform 10 Frisky Pony Kicks.

_____ _____ Lying on your back, knees bent, feet flat on floor, perform 10 Bench Presses with a medicine ball. (If medicine ball is too heavy, use a basketball and increase to 20 presses.)

_____ _____ Perform a Bar Hang, with chin above bar, for 7 seconds.

_____ _____ Perform 10 Push-Ups with good form in 45 seconds.

Fitness
Upper Body Strength
TASK CARD 3

Student Check	Teacher Check	CAN YOU?
_____	_____	Perform 20 Bench Dips with a light weight on your lap.
_____	_____	Perform 30 chair Push-Ups.
_____	_____	Do 6 overhand Pull-Ups.
_____	_____	Perform 15 regular Hop-Line Push-Ups followed by 10 clapping while in air over the line.
_____	_____	Perform 20 regular Push-Ups followed immediately by 10 triangle Push-Ups.

Fitness
Lower Body Strength
TASK CARD 1

Student Check	Teacher Check	CAN YOU?

_____ _____ Perform Wall-Sits for 30 seconds with back against the wall and arms crossed on chest.

_____ _____ Perform 45 alternating-foot Side Hops (left and right = 1) in 30 seconds.

_____ _____ Perform 10 Obstacle Jumps in 30 seconds with good form.

_____ _____ Perform Stretch Jumps to wall, alternating hand touches, for 30 seconds continuously. (Record the number of touches you made _____.) Remember to use good form and stretch arms completely upward.

_____ _____ Perform 30 double-foot Side Jumps over a 1-foot line in 30 seconds continuously.

Fitness
Lower Body Strength
TASK CARD 2

Student Check	*Teacher Check*	**CAN YOU?**
_____	_____	Perform Wall-Sits for 60 seconds with back against wall and arms crossed on chest.
_____	_____	Perform 60 alternating-foot Side Hops (left and right = 1) in 45 seconds.
_____	_____	Perform 15 Obstacles Jumps in 45 seconds with good form.
_____	_____	Perform Stretch Jumps at a wall, alternating hand touches, for 45 seconds continuously. (Record the number of touches you made _____.) Remember to use good form and stretch arms completely.
_____	_____	Perform 40 double-foot Side Jumps over a 1-foot line in 30 seconds continuously.

Fitness
Lower Body Strength
TASK CARD 3

Student Check	Teacher Check	CAN YOU?
_____	_____	Perform 30 single-leg Side Jumps over a 1-foot line in 45 seconds using your right leg. Try not to let the left leg touch down.
_____	_____	Perform 30 single-leg Side Jumps over a 1-foot line in 45 seconds using your left leg. Try not to let the right leg touch down.
_____	_____	Perform 15 double-leg Lateral Jumps over an object in 30 seconds.
_____	_____	Perform 60 seconds of continuous Front Box Jumping using good form. (Remember to keep the feet together when jumping and land softly with knees sightly bent.)
_____	_____	Perform 10 Ball Pick-Ups in 45 seconds.

Fitness
Abdominal Strength
TASK CARD 1

Student Check	Teacher Check	CAN YOU?
_____	_____	Lie on your back, feet flat on the floor, knees bent. Lift your head and neck up approximately 6 to 12 inches and wave to a friend for 10 seconds.
_____	_____	Repeat the above activity adding holding one leg in the air at the same time.
_____	_____	Do 10 bent-knee Sit-Ups, arms crossed over chest, partner holding feet.
_____	_____	Perform 10 (each) See-Saw Rows with partner. (Place soles of feet together, knees slightly bent, and row back and forth.)
_____	_____	Lie on your back, arms crossed over chest. Raise head and neck approximately 6 inches, hold; raise leg, knees slightly bent, approximately 12 inches; hold complete position for 15 seconds.

Fitness
Abdominal Strength
TASK CARD 2

Student Check	*Teacher Check*	**CAN YOU?**
_____	_____	Lie on your back, feet flat on the floor, knees bent. Lift your head and neck up approximately 6 to 12 inches and wave to a friend for 25 seconds.
_____	_____	Repeat the above activity adding holding both legs in the air at the same time, knees slightly bent.
_____	_____	Do 10 bent-knee Sit-Ups, arms crossed over chest.
_____	_____	Perform 10 (each) See-Saw Rows with partner while holding a medicine ball between you. (Place soles of feet together, knees slightly bent, and row back and forth.)
_____	_____	Assume a bent-knee Sit-Up position, partner holding feet. Hold a medicine ball in your arms and complete 10 Sit-Ups.

Fitness
Abdominal Strength
TASK CARD 3

Student Check	*Teacher Check*	**CAN YOU?**

_____ _____ Perform 10 V-Sit-Ups with good form.

_____ _____ Put your legs over a chair or bench so you are in a position with your hips directly under your knees. Lift head and shoulders up 10 times.

_____ _____ Sit with legs straight and back at a 45-degree angle, arms crossed over chest. Bring knees to chest, return to starting position without allowing legs to touch floor, 10 times.

_____ _____ Perform 15 bent-knee Sit-Ups. Each time you come up, pass a medicine ball to your partner. Remain up until partner passes the ball back to you, lie down with ball, and begin again.

_____ _____ Assume bent-knee Sit-Up position, arms on floor over head, holding a medicine ball. When coming up, pass ball to a partner standing 3 feet away. Partner passes back to you, lie down, and repeat 10 times.

BASIC AEROBIC ROUTINES (4–8)

Focus: Cardiovascular endurance

Equipment: Tape player, music

Description:

These basic aerobic routines are developed to present the student with a rhythmic exercise pattern using basic steps for a predetermined number of musical beats. Each of the "steps" listed reflects fundamental movements either previously learned or easily accomplished.

Procedure:

Transfer the routine as listed below onto a large piece of construction paper and post in the front of the room. The first time the routine is presented, demonstrate any new steps and have the students practice. Play the music, count the beats, and indicate to the students the "steps" they will be doing at that time. Arrange the students in a scatter formation and begin the routine.

Organization:

Do not stop the routine if a few students appear out of step. Provide individual assistance at a later time.

Sample Basic Routines:

Song: "America"; Artist: Neil Diamond; Capitol Records

EXERCISE	MEASURE	CUE
stretching	8	introduction
run in place	8	first heavy beat
Side Swings	8	"Far"
run in place	8	"Free"
Toe-Heel	8	"On the boat"
4-count toe touch	8	"Home"
rest	2	
Jumping Jacks	8	"Home"
rest	2	
run in place	4	heavy beat
Side Swing	8	"Everywhere"
run in place	8	"Got a dream"
stretching	8	"Today"
Can-Can Kicks	8	"Today"

FITNESS-ABILITY GROUP EXERCISES (4-8)

Focus: Cardiovascular fitness, muscular strength, flexibility

Equipment: Jump ropes, exercise list

Description:

An individual fitness activity for large groups. This activity allows for different levels of ability, progress, and motivation within whole classes while students work side by side with others of similar ability.

Procedure:

Divide students into small groups according to fitness levels. Assign a leader for each group, who calls out the muscle group to be exercised and the specific exercise selected from the provided list. Arrange each group in a different part of the facility and get ready to begin.

1. At the signal to start, all students jog 2 laps of the gym and return to their area.
2. When all have returned, give the signal to start exercise/activities.
3. Each group will perform the exercise called out by the leader for 30 seconds.
4. At the end of the 30-second period, the teacher says "Change" and the leader calls out another exercise.
5. After 3 exercises, each group jogs 2 laps and returns to its area.
6. Continue until all muscle groups have been exercised.

Organization:

1. Give each leader a copy of the exercise/activity card for their group.
2. Make sure all students know how to perform the exercises to be completed by their group.
3. Remind the students that they are exercising at their own pace, *not* for a specified number of sets.

Sample Exercise Activity Cards:

MUSCLE GROUP	ADVANCED	INTERMEDIATE	BEGINNER
abdominals	Crunches	Curl-Ups	¼ Curl-Ups
arms	Hop-Line	Bench Dips	Knee Push-Ups
legs	Rope Skipping	Side Leg Lifts	Treadmill

All Run 2 Laps

Muscle group	Advanced	Intermediate	Beginner
upper back	Wing Lifts (hold 8 counts)	Wing Lifts (hold 4 counts)	Wing Lifts (no hold)
arms	Bench-Dips	Triangle Push-Ups	Crab Walk
legs	Jump Rope	Jump Rope	Jump Rope

All Run 2 Laps

Muscle group	Advanced	Intermediate	Beginner
abdominals	Crunches	Curl-Ups	Curl-Ups
arms	Triangle Push-ups	Spider Push-Ups	Hop-Line Push-Ups

All Jump Rope for 2 Minutes

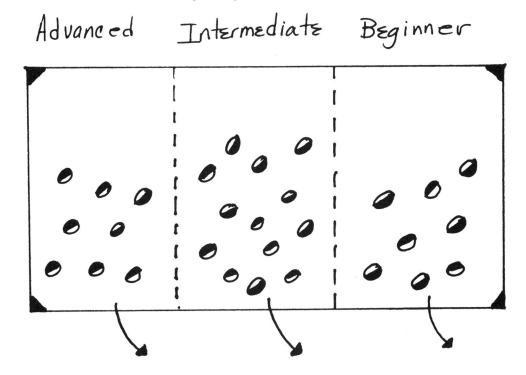

Advanced   Intermediate   Beginner

MELT-DOWN (4-8)

Focus: Increase overall fitness

Equipment: Cones, task cards

Description:

A fast-paced activity including a series of jogging laps interspersed with a variety of exercise/activities located at various stations around the facility. This activity keeps all students moving for the entire time period.

Procedure:

Assign students to groups according to the number of stations that have been set up; e.g., 6 stations = 6 groups. Assign each group to a station and get ready to begin.

1. On the start signal, the students begin to perform the exercise/activity at their station for a designated time period.
2. At the end of the time period, all students jog the perimeter of the facility for a predetermined number of laps.
3. Once the jogging is completed, students rotate clockwise to the next station and begin that exercise/activity.
4. Continue until all stations have been completed and finish with a slow jog/walk of 2 laps.

Modification:

Design task cards for each station with a specific exercise and designate the number of laps students are to jog. Then allow the students to work at their own pace. When allowing students to work on their own, provide continuous encouragement for them to stay on task.

Sample Activities and Time Frames:

Beginners: 20 to 30 seconds per station
Intermediates: 35 to 45 seconds per station
Advanced: 50 to 60 seconds per station

Number of Laps Between Stations:

End of first station: 5 laps
End of second station: 4 laps
End of third station: 3 laps
End of fourth station: 2 laps
End of remaining stations: 1 lap

Sample Exercise Activities:

Push-Ups	Crab Kicks	Kick Through
Curl-Ups	V-Ups	Crunches
Treadmill	Squat Thrust	Rope Skipping
Sit and Reach	Side Flex	Quad Stretch

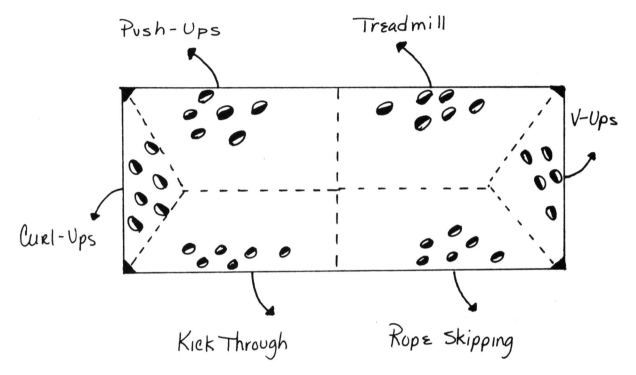

PROGRESSIVE CIRCUIT AEROBICS (4-8)

Focus: Cardiovascular endurance, muscular strength

Equipment: Tennis and playground balls, hand weights, chairs, task cards

Description:

A high intensity and motivational alternative to basic circuit training and aerobic exercise. This activity utilizes a series of exercise stations combined with sets of aerobic activity.

Procedure:

Arrange students in groups according to the number of exercise stations set up. (See "Basic Circuit Exercises.") Once the students know their assigned station, have them assume a scattered formation to perform the first aerobic activity.

1. On signal, students perform a selected aerobic routine.
2. At the conclusion of that routine, students move quickly to their assigned station and begin to perform the exercise/activity listed for 30 seconds.
3. At the conclusion of the exercise set, they perform a teacher/student-led aerobic activity for 45 seconds.
4. At the conclusion of the aerobic activity, they rotate to the next exercise/activity station and begin.
5. Continue until all stations have been completed and finish with 2 minutes of slow jogging, followed by 1 minute of walking.

Organization:

Students must be familiar with the aerobic routines(s) before performing this activity or the total value will be lost.

REVOLVING FITNESS (4-8)

Focus: Refine overall fitness, manipulative skills

Equipment: Beanbags, tennis balls and footballs, basket, playground mats, challenge cards

Description:

A relay-type activity that involves the entire class performing various challenges to score a point for their group.

Procedure:

Arrange the facility with five stations (mats) around the perimeter. At the center, spread out on the floor a set of challenge cards. Each challenge card corresponds to a station. Divide students into 6 groups with each student within the group given a letter; e.g., A B C D E F. Assign each group an area to use as "home base."

1. To begin, call out a letter and the student from each group with that letter runs to the center, takes a challenge card, and returns to his or her "home base."
2. All students in that group then run to that station.
3. The leader performs the activity, hands the card to the next person, and begins to jog 1 lap—ending up at the group's "home base."
4. Each person in the group performs the activity and then jogs.
5. The last person to get the card performs the activity, jogs, and returns the card to the center.
6. The first team to complete the station earns 5 points, second team earns 4, etc.
7. Continue until all groups have completed each challenge.

Organization:

1. Make several sets of laminated cards in different colors and color-code groups. Place the cards in a different order so that all groups do not end up at the same station at the same time.
2. Have a combination of fitness challenges as well as manipulative challenges in each color.

Sample Activities:

Fitness Challenges:

1. Run to the mats and all group members perform Push-Ups (for beginners, 20 seconds; intermediates, 30 seconds; advanced, 40 seconds).

2. Run to the mats and all group members perform Curl-Ups (for beginners, 30 seconds; intermediates, 45 seconds; advanced, 60 seconds).
3. Run to the jump ropes and jump for 30 seconds.
4. Do 25 Treadmills.
5. All group members run 2 laps of the facility.
6. Do 25 Squat Thrusts.

Manipulative Challenges:

1. Run to the basketballs and dribble 20 to 30 times in one spot.
2. Perform 10 Chest Passes with a partner.
3. Perform 10 Bounce Passes to a partner.
4. Perform a Figure-8 Pass through your legs 10 times.
5. Center the football to a partner 10 feet away, 5 times.
6. Toss a beanbag in the air, sit down, and catch it, 5 times.

BOX, BAND, AND BALL CIRCUIT (4–8)

Focus: Cardiovascular, coordination, muscular strength, endurance

Equipment: Stepping boxes, surgical tubing, jump ropes, various sized balls

Description:

An alternative fitness circuit using specialized pieces of equipment. This activity can be used in combination with aerobic routines, thus creating a fast-paced aerobic exercise period.

Procedure:

Set up stations depending upon the number of students in the class. Make certain there is one piece of equipment for each student/station. When setting up the stations, alternate between box, band, jump ropes, and balls. Divide students into groups depending upon the number of stations available. Assign each group to its starting station.

1. Begin with all students performing 2 minutes of an aerobic routine.
2. Give the signal to start. Have the beginning students perform the activity for 30 seconds; intermediate, 45 seconds; and advanced, 60 seconds.
3. At the end of the time, have the students rotate clockwise to the next station.
4. Continue the rotation until all stations have been completed and conclude with a 2-minute aerobic routine followed by a 1-minute walk cool-down.

Modification:

If there is not enough equipment for each student at the station, place jump ropes at each station and follow the modified format listed below:

1. Have the students perform the activities listed for each station. Those not using the specialized equipment are skipping rope. Have different rope-skipping tasks at each station.
2. An alternate method of rotation could be to have the student rotate to the next station when he or she completes the task at the previous station. When the student arrives at the next station, he or she skips rope until his or her turn to complete the activity.

Box Activities:

Jumping-box activities are designed to enhance lower body strength as well as balance and coordination skills. The construction of the box is simple. You need a box 8 to 12″ high × 24″ wide and 24 to 48″ long. Longer boxes may require some additional stabilization. They should be strong enough to hold a 150 to 200-pound individual. Both the top and bottom should be covered with a non-skid surface. Longer boxes allow more students to participate at one time, but may also be more difficult to transport. Many times lumber dealers will have excess materials they will donate.

1. Set-Ups: Have student face box. Step on box with right foot, bring left foot up on box, begin stepping down with right foot, then left foot. Make certain student maintains an erect posture. Repeat for designated time or number of repetitions.

2. Front Jumps: Have student face box and jump up with both feet and jump back down to start position. *Modification:* Have student jump forward off box, turn around, and repeat front jumping.

3. Lateral-Steps: Have student stand with right side to box. Step up laterally with right foot, then left foot. Step down with left foot, then right foot. Maintain erect posture during stepping. Student can repeat from the other side as well.

4. Lateral Jumps: Have student stand with right (left) side to box. Jump up with both feet, laterally, and then jump off the opposite side of box. Repeat activity. Make it continuous lateral jumping.

5. One-Foot Jump: Have student perform the Front Jump using only one foot. This is a difficult task for students to perform, especially if they have had a serious ankle injury and lost strength.

6. Jump Squats with/without Turn: Have student perform a Front Jump onto box, land in a Half-Squat (knees bent to 90 degrees). Immediately upon landing in squat, student explodes upward and off box, again landing in a Half-Squat position on the opposite side. After landing, student runs around to the other side, and repeats it so all students are going the same way. (You can run several students through this activity at the same time by using this approach.) Next, incorporate the turn. Have student perform the same activity, except when student explodes off the box, he or she performs a $\frac{1}{2}$ (180-degree) turn and lands facing the box. Student then repeats the activity going back the other way. *Modification:* This activity can also be performed with Lateral Jumps.

7. Jump and Catch: Have "passer" standing 4 to 6 feet from box, facing box with ball in hand. The "jumper" performs a Jump Squat onto the box. As student begins to explode off box, at the height of the jump the passer tosses the ball to the jumper. The jumper catches the ball and, immediately upon landing, tosses the ball back to the passer. All students in the group can participate by rotating the passer position. You may use any type of ball. A medicine ball is recommended for increases in upper-body fitness.

Band Activities:

For these activities you will need surgical tubing 6 to 9 feet in length, inner tubes from bicycles, or Dynabands™. If you find the bands are too long, have the students shorten them by simply adjusting their grip. By halfway through each repetition of the activity, the student should feel the resistance. If students are performing the activity too quickly and it looks as if the resistance is too low, have students adjust their grip.

Band activities are designed to enhance three fitness components: upper body, lower body, and abdominals. These activities can be used as a separate fitness activity or in conjunction with any other fitness circuit. Several activities have already been listed in the different fitness components to get you started. There are many others that can be used with some creativity.

Upper-Body Activities:

1. *Shoulder Abductions:* Have student stand with tubing under feet, holding it in right (left) hand, and extend arm sideways until it is shoulder height. *Slowly* lower arm back to starting position. Repeat using the opposite hand.

2. *Wing Stretches:* Student stands with arms shoulder height and elbow bent, holding tubing in hand approximately 1 foot apart. Perform Wing Stretches (horizontal adduction). Make certain to keep elbows shoulder height and return to starting position slowly.

3. *Rowing:* In a seated position with legs straight, place tubing around soles of feet. Grasping each side of tubing with arms extended, tubing taut, and elbows close to body, pull tubing toward torso. When hands are at chest, slowly return to starting position.

4. *The Archer:* In a standing position, wrap one end of tubing around each hand. Bringing both arms to shoulder height, extend right arm forward. Maintain this arm's position, slowly bring left arm back past cheek, and return slowly to starting position.

Lower-Body Activities:

1. *Leg Extensions:* Sit on floor, right leg bent with foot on floor, left extended, back straight. Place tubing around sole of left foot and grasp both ends with left hand. Bend knee to 90 degrees for starting position, and take up slack in tubing so it is taut. Slowly extend leg, keeping it off the floor. Once extended, slowly return to starting position. Repeat using the right leg.

2. *Quad Stretch:* Sit on floor with knees bent and feet 1 to 3 inches apart. Tie tubing around ankles so it is taut, but not too tight. Once tied, place tubing under right foot to stabilize it, and then around left ankle. Slowly extend left leg until it is even with right knee. Slowly return to starting position. Repeat using right leg. This activity must be done slowly for effectiveness as well as to keep the tubing from slipping.

Abdominal Activities:

1. *Curls:* Loop tubing around a stationary, heavy object or have a partner hold the ends of the tube. Assume a bent-knee Sit-Up position. Hands should be overhead holding the tube at the top of the head. Perform Curl-Up as normal, maintaining the hand position at the top of the head the entire time. It will take a couple of tries to get the tubing adjusted to the correct tension. You should be able to Curl-Up approximately three-fourths of the way and then slowly return to starting position. *Modifica-*

tion: Instead of holding tubing at head, place it in one hand and perform a complete Sit-Up, touching hands to knees. Slowly return to starting position.

2. *Rowing for Abdominals:* In a seated position, legs extended and back straight, loop tubing around soles of feet. Grasp both ends with hands. Bring legs 6 inches off the floor and bend knees to approximately 75 to 90 degrees. Take up slack in tubing so it is taut in bent position. Slowly extend legs, being careful not to let legs touch ground. Once extended, *slowly* return to starting position. Be careful to maintain good form by keeping the back straight and arms close to sides.

Ball Activities:

The medicine ball is a weighted ball designed to be used with various activities. One of the most beneficial uses is for strength training of the upper body. If you find they are too heavy for your students, then use a basketball and increase the number of repetitions or time frame.

1. *Trunk Twister:* Sitting on the floor with legs extended, student places the medicine ball directly behind his or her back. Twist to the left, pick up the ball, bring it around the front, twist to the right, and set the ball back in its starting position. Perform the activity from both sides of the body.

2. *Double-Unders:* Sitting on the floor with legs extended, student holds the ball in front. Raise legs off the ground, knees slightly bent. Roll the ball under legs from the left to the right and continue the process for a specific number of repetitions or time frame. Do not let legs touch the ground during the exercise. *Modification:* For students with greater abdominal strength, instead of rolling the ball, have them raise their legs higher, and pass the ball under the legs without it touching the ground.

3. *Drop and Catch:* Partner A lies on back, knees bent, feet flat on the floor. Partner B stands at the head of A, holding the ball over A's chest. On A's signal, B drops the ball, and A catches it before it lands on his or her chest. After the catch, A pushes the ball straight back up toward B to catch. Repeat for a specified number of repetitions or time period, then switch places. *Note:* Caution students to be very careful not to drop the ball until the receiver is ready so it does not land on the chest. *Modification:* For the first time, you may want to have the students perform it with a softer, lighter ball.

4. *Toss and Catch:* Standing 4 to 6 feet from partner, toss the medicine ball back and forth. Try not to let the ball touch the chest when catching.

5. *Front Catch:* Stand with the medicine ball between feet. Jump up with ball, and toss it to self. After catching the ball, place it back between feet and repeat activity.

6. Overhead Press: Student stands with feet approximately 3 to 6 inches apart and holds the ball in front of the body with both hands. Slowly "press" the ball overhead, hold for a count of three, then lower the ball to chest height. Repeat 5 to 7 times.

7. *Military Press:* Student lies down on back holding the ball with both hands on the chest. Straighten arms, hold for a count of three, then lower the ball to the chest. The ball should never rest on the chest, but just above it. Repeat 5 to 7 times. This activity can also be done in a standing position by having the student press the ball forward away from the body and return.

8. *Pullover Pass:* Student lies on back with knees bent, arms overhead on the floor. Hold the ball with both hands; keep the back fairly straight. Pass the ball to a partner, standing at the student's feet. The partner hands the ball back to the student to repeat the exercise. Repeat 5 to 7 times before switching places.

9. *Underhand Throw:* Stand in a squat position, holding the ball close to the ground. Keeping the back straight, student raises up and passes the ball underhand to a partner. Partner repeats the activity. Each individual should toss and catch 5 to 7 times.

10. *Over-Under:* Student sits on the floor with legs out in front. Lift the right leg and pass the ball under it from the inside. Then pass it over the top of the right leg, under the left leg, over the left leg, etc. Keep it going for 5 complete Over-Unders if possible. (This is actually a figure-8).

AEROBIC LINES (5-8)

Focus: Cardiovascular, muscular strength, endurance

Equipment: Cones, jump ropes

Description:

A high-level fitness activity combining aerobics and traditional exercises.

Procedure:

Students are placed in lines of six each behind a set of cones.

1. Begin the activity with 1 minute of aerobic movements with students in their lines.
2. Following the aerobic movements, begin 20 seconds of Push-Ups (use individual variations).
3. At the conclusion of the 20-second exercise, have students jog around the cones clockwise.
4. After students return to their line positions, begin the next exercise. Continue until all exercises are completed.
5. Conclude with 1 minute of aerobics and a 1-minute cool-down.

Sample Routine:

1. Aerobic Movement
2. Push-Up Variations
3. Jog
4. Bench Dips
5. Jog
6. Jump Rope
7. Jog
8. Kick Through
9. Jog
10. Aerobic Movement
11. Cool-Down

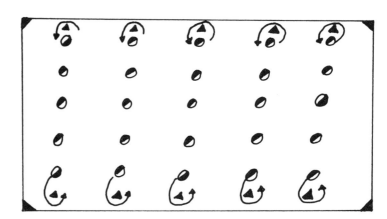

130

FUN AND FITNESS OLYMPICS (5-8)

Focus: Enhance general fitness levels, coordination, movement

Equipment: As needed for stations, score card, pencils

Description:

A diversified fitness activity that provides personal challenges in both traditional and nontraditional activities.

Procedure:

Set up a 10-station circuit to include skill-based tasks and fitness enhancement tasks. Make sure there is enough equipment at each station to accommodate the largest group as they move through. Divide students into groups of 3 to 4 each. Demonstrate each activity, if needed. Give a score card and pencil to each group and assign them to a beginning station.

1. At the start signal, students begin performing the activity at their stations, keeping track of their score.
2. After 1 minute give the stop signal and ask the students to total up their group's points and record the total on their score card.

3. Have students rotate clockwise and prepare to begin the next station.

4. Continue until all stations have been completed.

5. Have students total up their points and determine which group has the highest total.

Sample Stations and Scoring:

1. *Hula Hoop Twist:* Keep a hula hoop moving around any body part; 2 points for each 5 consecutive turns.

2. *Double-Unders:* Perform consecutive double-unders; 2 points for each consecutive 3.

3. *Curl-Ups:* 1 point for each completed Curl-Up.

4. *Hurdler:* Jump over the hurdle; 2 points for each 5 consecutive jumps without a miss. (To make the hurdle, stretch a rope between two chairs at the height where the majority of students will be successful.)

5. *Crab Walk:* Crab Walk for a distance of 15 feet; 1 point for reaching the 15-foot mark and an additional point for moving back to the starting line.

6. *Ball Dribble:* Dribble a ball around a figure-8 course; 1 point for each complete rotation.

7. *Balloon Volley:* Perform a "set" volley; 1 point for each consecutive 5 volleys.

8. *Push-Ups:* 1 point for each Push-Up completed.

9. *Rope-Skipping Tricks:* Perform various rope-skipping steps; 2 points for each 5 successful jumps. Add 10 points if you do 5 or more different steps.

10. *Ball Hop:* With an $8\frac{1}{2}$-inch ball between the knees, hop to a line 10 feet away; 2 points for reaching the line without dropping the ball and an additional 3 points for returning successfully.

Modifications:

1. Instead of a group approach, try having individuals keep their own score. After several times through this activity, have students note their progress.

2. Organize this activity as a field day or track meet. Instead of having all students perform each station, let them pick five of the ten.

Fun and Fitness Olympics Score Card

Name: _____ Date: _____

Team: _____

Record your total points for each event:

1. Hula Hoop Twist _____

2. Double-Unders _____

3. Curl-Ups _____

4. Hurdler _____

5. Crab Walk _____

6. Ball Dribble _____

7. Balloon Volley _____

8. Push-Ups _____

9. Rope-Skipping Tricks _____

10. Ball Hop _____

TOTAL POINTS _____

TEAM PREDICTION (5-8)

Focus: Cardiovascular, endurance, muscular strength, cooperation

Equipment: Beanbags, jump ropes, balloons, score cards, pencils

Description:

An advanced version of the "Individual 60-Second Prediction" that uses group scores instead of individuals'. Groups of students are presented with various fitness and skill challenges and are asked to predict their scores on each of the challenges.

Procedure:

Arrange five or more stations, allowing enough room among them for groups of 4 to 7 students to participate safely at one time. Arrange students into groups to equal the number of stations you have set up. This is a good time to use an alternative method of groups, such as birthday months, shoe size, etc., in order to get a variety of skill/fitness levels represented in each group. After groups have been assigned, give each team a score card and pencil and have them go to a beginning station.

1. Give the ready signal and allow students 30 to 45 seconds to discuss and estimate what their results will be at that station. They should write their prediction at this time.
2. Give the start signal to begin the activity. The activity should last for 3 minutes.
3. After the 3 minutes of activity, have the students stop and record their actual score.
4. Continue until each group has completed each station.
5. Have students discuss and calculate their group results.

Organization:

Provide enough time for students to discuss, record, and calculate their scores; e.g., 45 to 60 seconds are enough between stations and approximately 3 minutes at the end of the activity.

Sample Stations:

1. *Push-Ups* (individual variations using regular, spider, hop-line, or other modifications): How many can the team complete in 3 minutes?
2. *Curl-Ups* (regular, modified, partner, or crunches): How many can the team complete in 3 minutes?
3. *Beanbag Collection:* How many beanbags can the team collect in 3 minutes? *Organization:* Place a large number of beanbags or other small objects at one end of the facility. The group lines up in traditional relay formation at the opposite end. Students run one at a time, take one (allow them to take two

134

if you have enough) object and return to the group. Upon their return, the next person goes.

4. ***Ball Jump:*** How many trips can be made by the group in 3 minutes? *Organization:* The group is lined up in traditional relay formation. The first person places a playground ball between his or her knees and hops to a line 30 feet away, takes the ball in his or her hands, and runs back to the line. Upon his or her return, the next person begins.

5. ***Double-Unders:*** How many double-unders, with a single rope, can the group make in 3 minutes? *Organization:* If your students are not proficient at this skill, modify the activity to fit the skill level of the group.

Organization:

Let the students determine if one person in the group will do Push-Ups, Curl-Ups, or Double-Unders at one time or if the group will do them at once. Either way the *group total* is recorded.

Sample Team Prediction Score Card:

Team Name: _____

ACTIVITY	PREDICTION	ACTUAL	TOTAL
Beanbag Collection			
Ball Jump			
Double-Unders			
Curl-Ups			
Push-Ups			

POINT CHALLENGE (6-8)

Focus: Increase overall fitness, coordination, motor skill

Equipment: As needed for challenges, task cards

Description:

This is an exciting and challenging activity that involves ten stations, each with a different skill challenge. Some require cooperation, while others measure individual skills. Students spend a predetermined time at each station and record the number of points scored.

Procedure:

Using available equipment, arrange ten stations around the facility. Each station should have a task card listing the challenge and the scoring for that station. Have students get a partner (or in groups of 4) and go to a beginning station.

1. On the start signal, students begin the first challenge. Each partner should perform the activity for 1 minute.
2. At the conclusion of 1 minute, give the change signal and the other partner begins the challenge for 1 minute.
3. After the time period is up, have the students record their points and rotate clockwise to the next station.
4. After all stations have been completed, the students total their scores. Determine the top 25 percent, etc.

Organization and Motivation:

1. Set a goal of reaching 2,000 points per individual or per group.
2. Arrange the stations to place emphasis on the various components of fitness; e.g., put Speed Jump, Footsie, and Ball Hop following each other to provide for continuous cardiovascular exercise.
3. Increase or decrease the point goal depending on the ability of each class. Frustration by setting goals too high can cause students not to put forth appropriate effort.

Sample Challenge Stations and Points:

STATIONS	SCORING	NOTE
Foxtail Catch	3 points for catching end; 2 for middle; 1 for ball	toss between end, 2 for middle, and partners 1 for the ball
Volleybird Hit	1 point for each hit to a partner	toss between partners

Curl-Up Toss	1 point for each hit to a partner	standing partner tosses ball to person in Curl-Up
Footsie	1 point for each jump	
Speed Jump (Jump Rope)	1 point for each jump	
Squish Squash	1 point for each volley	between partners
Spin Jammer	1 point for each finger pop up	
Rocket Balls	1 point for each shot to a wall and catch	
Play Bouys	1 point for each round trip	
Ball Drop	1 point for each catch	partner drops a ball and other partner tries to catch it

3

Skill Challenges and Motivators

Skill Challenges and Motivators

Students at all grade levels are motivated by a challenge, but it is particularly important to be able to provide developmentally appropriate challenges for the elementary and middle-level student. At these levels students are being introduced to and refining basic skills leading towards recreational activities that may be participated in throughout their lives. Providing activities that reinforce basic skills, while combining them with various challenges, increases the interest as well as the skill level of individuals.

The activities in Section 3 provide methods to teach and enhance several sports skills, as well as provide a means to combine these skills with meaningful fitness activities. In this section you will find activities divided into the areas of "skill challenges," "emphasis station activities," and "lead-up activities."

The skill-challenge activities are designed to provide unique activities to challenge and motivate students in specific sports activities. The activities will provide variations of basic skills and are introduced at three levels. Start the students at the first level and have them proceed through all three levels. Hopefully, all students can be successful at the first level with minimum difficulty, and as they progress it will take more skill and work to complete. When completed, they will have refined the basic sports skills and enhanced other areas of importance for good performance; eye-hand coordination, balance, eye-foot coordination, and reaction time are just several objectives that can be accomplished through the skills-challenge activities.

The station-type activities provide yet another way to learn and enhance specific skills. In these activities there are task cards that allow the students to be self-directed in their learning. When using the task cards, it is recommended that you copy the cards (a different color for each sport), laminate them, and save the originals.

There are also lead-up activities with several of the sports. These activities are designed to refine specific skills while combining them in a game-type format.

In keeping with our previous sections, these activities are just the beginning of what can be done with various sport skills and activities. Use your imagination to create more activities.

Basic Skills and Fitness

MOVEMENT WITH A PURPOSE (K-2)

Focus: Reinforce basic locomotor skills, shapes, colors, numbers, and letters

Equipment: Number, letter and shape carpet squares (or laminated sheets with appropriate symbols), cones

Description:

An activity designed to provide students reinforcement in learning numbers, shapes, colors, and basic locomotor skills.

Procedure:

1. Set up the shape, number, and letter objects in the middle of the area. Place cones to make a square perimeter. (See diagram below.)
2. Scatter the objects around the inside of the playing area.
3. Have each student identify one as his or her home base and stand on/beside it.
4. Call out a locomotor movement. All students move in a clockwise direction toward the perimeter and perform the movement.
5. Call out a shape, color, number, letter, etc., and the student must find it and stand on it. More than one person may occupy a space.
6. Then call out the next locomotor movement.
7. Continue until the students tire or you want to move on to another activity.

Homework Assignments:

Have each student locate at home an object that fits a particular description. For example: List four things in your house that are square; or red; or have letters on it; etc. Depending upon the age level, parents might need to be involved.

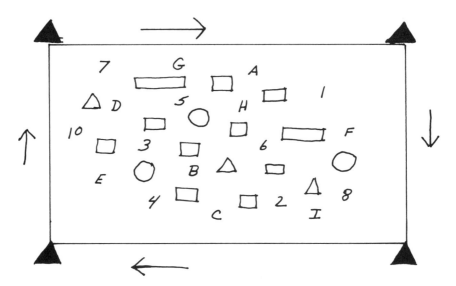

PUZZLE MANIA (2-6)

Focus: Fine motor skills, basic motor skills, and healthy heart information

Equipment: Puzzles

Description:

Designed to give students information about how to have a healthy heart through the use of puzzles. It will also refine basic locomotor skills and enhance the use of fine motor skills through puzzle building.

Procedure:

1. Set up the puzzles at one end of the playing area in relay formation (one puzzle for each team).
2. Divide students into five to seven teams at the opposite end of the playing area (standard relay formation). There should be no more than five on a team, if possible.
3. On the "go" signal, the first player runs to get a puzzle piece, comes back to the starting point, and touches the next person. This continues until all puzzle pieces are picked up.
4. When the last puzzle piece arrives, the students put together the puzzle to find out a message concerning a healthy heart.
5. Depending upon the age of the students, you could have a brief discussion about the message or assign it as homework.
6. Have the students take apart the pieces, turn the pieces upside down, and rotate one team to the right so they will have a new puzzle.
7. On the second round, the students take a puzzle piece to the opposite end and run back (just the opposite of round one).
8. This continues until all pieces are at the opposite end. The teams again construct the puzzle and find another message.
9. Continue the activity until all groups have had time to read all five to seven messages.

Modifications and Organization:

1. With younger students, you might want to consider having only one or two messages for each day. This will give you time to discuss the importance of each message.
2. Have older students write down the messages and later write a paragraph about each message as a homework assignment. This could be done as a group assignment or individually.
3. **Construction of puzzles:** This can be elaborate or simple, depending upon the amount of time you want to invest.

143

a. Draw a heart on a 9 × 12 piece of white paper. Inside the heart write the message. Laminate it, then cut it into 5 to 7 pieces depending upon the number you want. It is suggested if you use all white paper, you code the back so the pieces don't get mixed up.

b. Repeat "a," putting the same message on several different colors.

c. Repeat "a," putting a different message on a different color of paper.

4. If you put a different message on each color, you could then modify the activity. Put all the puzzle pieces in a big circle in the middle of the playing area. Assign each group a specific color and have them run to find their color and bring it back.

5. **Sample messages:** The following are only suggestions. Use your imagination or the class material you want your students to learn.

"Cardio" means "heart"/"Respiratory" means "lungs"

RHR = resting heart rate: The number of times our heart beats in 1 minute when completely relaxed

MHR = maximum number of times our heart beats in 1 minute

Exercise regularly/Eat sensibly/Limit your intake of junk food

Aerobic activity 3 to 5 times a week

Monitor blood pressure

Reduce stress

A stronger heart can pump more blood to carry more oxygen and give more energy

Oxygen-rich blood is bright red in color/Oxygen-poor blood is more bluish in color

BASIC APPARATUS SKILLS (3-5)

Focus: Improve fitness while increasing movement skills

Equipment: Hula hoops, wands, benches, balance beams, paddles, balls, climbing ropes, scooters, parachute, bounce boards, beanbags, task cards

Description:

Keeping to the comprehensive skill and fitness development format, students perform developmentally appropriate movements and skills on various pieces of equipment. Students progress through the tasks at their own pace. The tasks are arranged for six weeks of bilateral, six of unilateral, and six of cross-lateral work. (For activities involving rope skipping and individual tug-of-war ropes, see specific sections for those apparatus.)

Procedure:

Arrange three stations each day. Place the task cards on the wall behind each station and show students how to correctly perform the activity. As the students begin, move about the facility to reinforce and instruct students in proper technique. After 10 minutes, rotate students to the next station.

Sample Activities:

1. Hula Hoop:

grade 3

- Twirl hoop on as many different body parts as you can.
- Twirl on one arm, try to change from one arm to the other.
- Jump rope with hoop. Jump forward, backward, and sideward.
- Move in different ways through a hoop held by a partner.
- Move in different ways through a hoop held horizontally to the floor.
- Roll the hoop and run along side.
- Roll the hoop with reverse spin and kick it up to you.
- Roll the hoop with reverse spin and go through it as it comes back.
- Roll the hoop with reverse spin, kick it up, catch it on your arm, and begin an arm spin.

grade 4

- Twirl a hoop on as many different body parts as you can.
- Twirling a hoop on one arm, try to change the hoop from one arm to the other.
- Roll hoop and run along side of it, pick it up on your arm, and begin to twirl while running.
- Toss the hoop to a partner who catches it on one arm and begins an arm spin.

- Play catch with a partner using two or more hoops.
- Find four ways to get on the other side of a moving hoop.
- Roll the hoops with reverse spin and see how many times a partner can go through it before it stops.

grade 5

- Spin a hoop on your leg.
- Spin the hoop on your ankle and jump over it with the other foot.
- Spin the hoop on your right arm, toss it in the air, catch it on your left hand, and begin a spin. Repeat after three spins.
- While spinning a hoop around your arm or leg, attempt to change hoop from one partner to another.
- Roll a hoop with reverse spin, kick it up, have a partner catch it, and begin an arm spin.

2. **Wand:**

grade 3

- Isometric push-pull.
- Thread-the-needle V-sit.
- Shoulder dislocate.
- Jump stick.
- A "Slave Twist."
- A "Wand Twirl."
- Toss to a partner and catch with a regular grip.
- Toss to a partner and catch with a reverse grip.

grade 4

- Shoulder dislocate.
- Wand balance on one finger.
- Jump stick.
- Back scratcher.
- Toss to a partner and catch with a mixed grip.
- Perform a sit and reach. Hold reach position for 15 seconds.
- Hold wand with palm of one hand and duck/twist under.

grade 5

- Shoulder dislocate.
- Wand whirl.
- Jump stick.

- Balance wand in the palm of hand, toss up, clap hands, and catch.
- Balance wand on toe, toss up, and catch.
- Toss wand in the air, turn 360 degrees, and catch.

3. **Bench:**

grade 3

- Pulls: prone, supine, side position.
- Crouch-jump length of bench.
- Straddle jump.
- Jump dismount with half turn.
- Crouch-jump with one hand and one foot.
- Stand on bench, do a straddle jump off and back on.

grade 4

- Crouch jump.
- Crouch jump using one hand and two feet.
- Crouch jump using one hand and one foot.
- Jump dismount with full turn.
- Pulls: prone, supine, side position.
- Straddle jump along bench and do a jackknife dismount.

grade 5

- Crouch jump (both hands).
- Crouch jump using one hand and two feet.
- Crouch jump using one hand and one foot.
- Forward roll on bench, stand, and perform a jackknife dismount.
- Pull along bench, stand, and perform a 180-degree turn with splits.

4. **Balance Beam:**

grade 3

- Walk forward and pass under a wand held 3′ high. Walk backwards.
- Walk forward, arms sideward, palms down, with eraser on the back of each hand.
- Walk backward, arms sideward, palms up, with eraser on each hand.
- Walk forward to middle of beam, kneel on one knee, straighten right leg forward until knee is straight. Rise and walk to end of beam. Do with other knee.
- Walk to center of beam, do a front scale, turn, and walk off backwards.
- Walk to center, sit, do a V-sit, stand, and walk off.
- Bunny Hop the length of the beam.

grade 4

- Cat walk.
- Bunny Hop on beam.
- Stand on right foot, eyes closed, and count number of seconds balance is maintained. Do on left foot.
- Walk forward, hands on hips, pass under wand held 3′ high. Walk backwards.
- Walk to the center, do a push-up, stand, and walk off.
- Walk forward to center, kneel, place a beanbag on your head, stand, and walk off.
- With a beanbag on your head, walk to center, step over a wand 15″ above beam, do a full turn, and walk off.
- Using a side step, repeat the last three activities.

grade 5

- Hop on right foot the full length of beam. Do with left foot.
- Hop on right foot the full length of beam, turn around, and hop back. Do with left foot.
- Walk to middle, balance on one foot (scale), turn around on this foot, and walk backward to end of beam.
- Walk to middle, do a V-sit, rise, and walk to end of beam.
- Walk to middle, kneel on one knee, place eraser on top of head, rise, turn around, and walk backward to end of beam.
- Walk to center, do several push-ups, stand, and walk off.
- Walk on beam with eyes closed. Use a spotter.
- Walk down the beam, kneel at end, and do a forward roll dismount (roundoff dismount, etc.).
- With partner starting at each end of beam, both walk forward and pass in the middle.
- With a partner, do a wheelbarrow the length of the beam, switch positions, turn, and go back. (At first the partner holding the legs can walk with feet on the ground, straddling beam, then progress to both people on the beam.)

5. **Paddle and Ball: (For additional activities see Racquet Sports)**

grade 3

- Balance ball on paddle.
- Roll ball around edges of paddle without it falling off.
- Bounce ball off paddle in air without it touching the floor.
- Bounce ball off paddle in air and catch it with other hand.
- Dribble ball with paddle from stationary position.

grade 4

- Balance ball on paddle.
- Roll ball on edges of paddle.
- Bounce ball off paddle without it touching the floor.
- Bounce ball off paddle and catch with other hand.
- Dribble ball from stationary position.
- Dribble ball from moving position.

grade 5

- Roll ball on edges of paddle.
- Bounce ball off paddle without it touching the floor.
- Dribble ball from a stationary position; moving position.
- Alternate bouncing the ball in air and on the floor.
- Bounce ball off paddle into the air and "catch" it with paddle. ("Give" with the paddle.)

6. **Climbing Rope:**

grade 3

- Jump and hang.
- Pull-ups from knees.
- Jump and swing to target.
- Hanging, lift with legs together.
- Climb and lower from lying position using a following grip.
- Climb, using a following grip, to a height of 15 feet.
- Jump, hang, and do bicycle movements.
- Climb, using a cross-over grip, to a height of 15 feet.
- Do an inverted hang with feet wrapped around the rope.

grade 4

- From a bench, hold on to the rope, swing out, and jump into a target.
- Climb and lower from a lying position, keep legs straight.
- Hang inverted with feet wrapped around rope.
- "Skin the Cat."
- An "L" sit.
- Climb as high as you can without using your feet.

grade 5

- Do pull-ups using two ropes.
- Climb, using a following grip, to an approved height.

- An "L" sit using two ropes.
- "Skin the Cat" with two ropes.
- A "dislocate" using two ropes.
- A "back L sit."

7. Scooter:

grade 3

- Sitting, push and pull with feet simultaneously through series of cones.
- Kneeling, push and pull with hands simultaneously through cones.
- Lying, use butterfly stroke. Increase distances.
- Partners: one sits, one pushes with hands on rider's shoulders. (Pusher never loses contact.)
- Relay races using first three activities above.
- Kneeling, push-pull with right or left hand only.
- Sitting, push-pull with right or left leg only.
- With right hand and knee on scooter, push with left. Reverse.
- Lie on scooter, push with right hand and foot. Reverse.
- Relay races with partners; one pushes and other rides.
- Sitting, push-pull with alternate feet.
- Kneeling, push-pull with alternate hands.
- Lying, push-pull with alternate foot and hand together.
- Scooter Basketball.

grade 4

- Sitting, push-pull with feet simultaneously through cones.
- Kneeling, push-pull with hands simultaneously through series of cones.
- Lying, use butterfly stroke. Increase distances.
- Relay races.
- Partners: one sits, one pushes with hands on rider's shoulders. (Pusher never loses contact.)
- Kneeling, push-pull with right or left hand only.
- Sitting, push-pull with right or left leg only.
- With right hand and knee on scooter, push with left. Reverse.
- Lying on scooter, push with right hand and foot. Reverse.
- Relay races with partners; one pushes and other rides.
- Sitting, push-pull with alternate feet.
- Kneeling, push-pull with alternate hands.
- Lying, push-pull with alternate foot and hand together.
- Scooter Basketball.

grade 5

- Sitting, push-pull with feet simultaneously through cones.
- Kneeling, push-pull with hands simultaneously through cones.
- Lying, use butterfly stroke. Increase distances.
- Relay races.
- Partners: one sits, one pushes with hands on rider's shoulders. (Pusher never loses contact.)
- Kneeling, push-pull with right or left hand only.
- Sitting, push-pull with right or left leg only.
- With right hand and knee on scooter, push with left. Reverse.
- Lying on scooter, push with right hand and foot. Reverse.
- Relay races with partners; one pushes and other rides.
- Sitting, push-pull with alternate feet.
- Kneeling, push-pull with alternate hands.
- Lying on scooter, push-pull with alternate foot and hand together.
- Scooter Basketball.

8. **Parachute:**

grade 3

- Exercises: toe touch, curl-ups.
- Shake with both hands.
- Dome making.
- In a circular motion, grapevine step.
- Number exchange game.
- Mushroom Release.
- Dorsal lifts; V-sit.
- Shake and pull with right or left hand.
- Dome making with right or left hand.
- Circular motion: hop, run, walk, skip.
- Popcorn.
- Hip walk, scooter.
- Cross-grip shake and pull.
- Cross-grip dome making.
- Running Number Game.

grade 4

- Exercises: dorsal lifts, curl-ups.
- Shake with both hands.
- Dome making.

- Grapevine step, both directions.
- Team Ball.
- V-sit, backward pulls.
- Shake and pull with right or left hand.
- Dome making with right or left hand.
- Circular motion activities.
- Circular Dribble Game.
- Popcorn.
- Dorsal lifts, backward pulls.
- Cross-grip shake and pull.
- Cross-grip dome making.

grade 5

- Exercises: dorsal lifts, curl-ups.
- Shake with both hands.
- Dome making.
- Grapevine step, both directions.
- Team Ball.
- V-sit, backward pulls.
- Shake and pull with right or left hand.
- Dome making with right or left hand.
- Circular motion activities.
- Popcorn.
- Dorsal lifts, backward pulls.
- Cross-grip shake and pull.
- Running Number Game.

9. **Bounce Board:**

grade 3

- Jump on both feet doing half turns. Do turns in both directions.
- Jump and do full turns.
- Make half turns right and left while hopping on center with right foot, left foot.
- Toss beanbag with right or left hand, hop on right or left foot.
- Knee Slap—Heel Tap.
- Jump 10 times and dismount with a half turn.
- Do any combination of jumps and dismount with a full turn.
- Dismount with different body shapes; e.g., jackknife, stretch.
- Dismount with a jump through a hoop held by a partner.

grade 4

- Dismount with a stretch jump followed by a forward roll.
- Dribble a ball while jumping.
- Using a playground ball, play catch with a partner while you jump and partner stands in front of the board.
- Toss a beanbag from one hand to the other while jumping.
- Juggle while jumping.
- Dismount with a jump through a hoop held by a partner.
- Jump and do full turns on the board.
- Do continuous knee slap—heel taps on the board.

grade 5

- Jump with a full turn every other jump.
- Juggle while jumping. Try straddle jumps.
- Dismount with a jump into a hoop, followed by a forward roll.
- Dismount with a half turn, followed by a backward roll.
- Dismount with a straddle jump, followed by a combination tumbling move; e.g., straddle roll to round off.

10. Beanbag:

grade 3

- Toss and catch—one hand, both hands, back of hands. Attempt from sitting and standing positions.
- Toss from side to side. Do from standing and sitting positions.
- Toss overhead, turn, and catch. Toss no higher than head.
- Balance beanbag on instep; walk, hop, swing leg forward and backward.
- Balance beanbag on head; walk, hop, run, skip, and jump.
- Toss from hands behind back overhead and catch in front.
- Toss around body, under the legs, behind head/back, and catch.
- Juggle with 2 beanbags/3 beanbags (use juggling cubes if available).
- Toss to a partner using different throwing motions; e.g., football throw, underhand pitch, overhand pitch.
- Toss, touch the floor, and catch.
- Toss, run forward, clap hands, and catch (keep toss low).

grade 4

- Toss beanbag from foot to hand. Clap twice before you catch it.
- With a partner toss back and forth as quickly as possible. Can you do 10 tosses in 15 seconds?

- Lie on your back and toss/catch from various positions; e.g., foot to hands, toss, roll over, and catch.
- From a sitting position, toss, stand up, and catch.
- Juggle 2 or 3 beanbags (use juggling cubes if available).
- Toss, touch the floor, clap hands, and catch. Toss no higher than 12 inches above your head.
- Place beanbag between your feet, kick up, and catch.

grade 5

- Toss overhead and catch behind your back.
- With the bag between your feet, kick up and catch.
- Move the beanbag around your body as quickly as possible: go around your back, between your legs, etc.
- Lie down, toss beanbag in the air, stand up, and catch.
- With a partner, toss two beanbags back and forth. Try it with each of you having two beanbags—toss at the same time.
- With one partner standing still, the other person runs in a large circle tossing the beanbag back and forth.
- Stand back to back—five feet apart—toss overhead and the other person catch it. (Call out "toss" when you toss it so your partner knows it is coming.)
- Toss the beanbag in the air, sit down, and catch it.
- Toss to a partner using feet.

Basketball Skills and Fitness

Basic Basketball Skills (K-2)

Focus: Basic ball skills

Equipment: Junior basketballs, playground balls

Description:

Students individually work on basic ball-handling skills using a basketball as a motivator. Emphasis is placed on bouncing (dribbling), passing and catching, and shooting.

Procedure:

Give each student an appropriate size ball (junior basketball or $8\frac{1}{2}''$ playground ball). After students have a ball ask them to spread out throughout the facility. Direct the students to perform the following tasks. *Note:* These are only a few basic ball skills. A basic progression of skills should be taught prior to introducing these tasks.

1. Bounce the ball and catch.
2. Bounce the ball with two hands while remaining in one place.
3. Bounce with one hand.
4. Bounce with one hand while remaining in one place.
5. Pass to a partner—anyway you can.
6. Pass to a partner using a chest pass, a bounce pass, an overhead pass.
7. Pass to a partner while he or she is moving.
8. Using a low basket (K–1, 5 foot; 2, $6\frac{1}{2}$ foot) shoot the ball. Work on proper form: elbows in, knees slightly bent, push up with good release, and follow through.

Motivation:

1. While the basketball itself is a great motivator, success is an even greater one. Modify all activities, **especially shooting,** to ensure success of all students.
2. Do not put a great deal of emphasis on lead-up activities to playing the game of basketball. Teach and refine skills for their own sake. These skills form the basis for many other activities.

BASKETBALL SKILLS CHALLENGES (K-2)

Focus: Refinement of skills

Equipment: Playground balls (7" to $8\frac{1}{2}$"), instructor check list

Description:

A variety of skill challenges designed to motivate students and provide alternative methods to practice the skills. Both traditional and nontraditional activities are utilized to provide success opportunities for students at all ability levels.

Procedure:

1. Provide each student with a ball.
2. Arrange students for a quick check off. (See "Organization" section below.)
3. Demonstrate the activities as necessary.
4. Allow students time to practice the challenges.
5. Begin checking off students who can complete each challenge. (See "Organization" section for suggestions.)
6. After the first level has been completed, move each student to the next level.
7. Provide certificates after each level for completion and positive reinforcement.

Organization:

1. If you have the students arranged in typical squad formation (alphabetically), this will allow you to watch more of them at one time and check off the skills completed.
2. When checking off the skills, it is sometimes easier to mark only the student who **cannot** complete the challenge.
3. If you find the challenges are too difficult (more than 30% of the class not able to complete), modify to a lower level for greater success.

Basketball Skill Challenge
Beginning Level

In a Sitting Position:
CAN YOU?

Toss and catch to self 3 times without missing.

Hold ball, head high, drop it, and catch it after first bounce.

Bend knees, feet flat on floor, roll ball in front of feet and around under legs with control 3 times.

In a Kneeling Position:
CAN YOU?

Hold ball shoulder height, drop it, and catch it after first bounce.

Bounce and catch ball to self 3 times without missing.

Toss and catch ball to self 3 times without missing.

In a Standing Position:
CAN YOU?

Toss and catch a ball in front of your body 3 times without missing.

Bounce and catch a ball 3 times without missing.

Toss-clap and catch the ball one time without missing.

Toss-turn $\frac{1}{4}$ way, catch one time without missing.

Roll the ball in a circle without losing control.

Toss ball against the wall and catch it 3 times in a row.

Completion Date: _____

Teacher Signature: _____

Basketball Skill Challenge
Intermediate Level

In a Standing Position:
CAN YOU?

Toss and catch a ball in front of your body 6 times without missing.

Dribble ball in place 5 to 10 times without missing.

Toss-clap and catch the ball 3 times without missing.

Toss-turn $\frac{1}{2}$ way, catch one time without missing.

Chest pass the ball against the wall and catch it 6 times in a row.

Catch a ball tossed to you while you are walking toward it.

While walking forward toss a ball to someone else so he or she can catch it.

Completion Date: _____

Teacher Signature: _____

Basketball Skill Challenge
Advanced Level

In a Standing Position:
CAN YOU?

Chest pass back and forth with a partner 3 to 5 feet away 10 times successfully. (Each person passes five times.)

Dribble ball forward 5 to 10 feet without losing control.

Toss-turn $\frac{3}{4}$ way, catch one time without missing.

Chest pass the ball against the wall and catch it 6 times in a row.

Toss and catch with a partner while both of you are walking forward 3 times each.

Completion Date: _____

Teacher Signature: _____

BASKETBALL EMPHASIS STATIONS (4–8)

Focus: A variety of challenging activities for each skill level

Equipment: Basketball, markers, hula hoops, student cards

Description:

Students are divided into four groups and assigned to a specific emphasis station. Students work individually or in groups to accomplish the assigned tasks.

Procedure:

1. Assign students to emphasis stations.
2. Students spend 10 minutes at each station, moving from the beginning level to the ending task.
3. After completing a station, you may check it off on the individual student cards.

Modification:

1. For younger students, design emphasis stations to include basic skills using a basketball or playground ball to accomplish theme tasks of moving, striking, and shooting.
2. Create additional challenges for students who progress through the station. In addition, lower-level challenges should be made available in order to allow all students to experience success.

Basketball Skills
Station 1, Dribbling

- Perform a cross-over dribble, while remaining stationary, for 30 seconds.

- While sitting in a chair, bounce a ball in a half circle without missing; go a full circle without missing.

- While sitting, bounce a ball halfway around a chair, stop it, and bounce it back the other way.

- From a bridge position, bounce the ball under your body 10 times first with the dominate hand. Perform with nondominate hand.

- Dribble through a series of cones with dominate hand and back with non-dominate hand.

- Do a cross-over back and forth between your legs, while remaining stationary, 20 to 30 seconds.

- Repeat above challenge, moving forward for 10 steps; backwards 10 steps.

Basketball Skills Station 2, Ball Handling/Coordination

- Quickly pass the ball around your body for 20 seconds without losing control.

- Repeat for 30 to 45 seconds.

- Repeat, timing how long, up to two minutes, without losing control.

- Perform a figure-eight rotation between legs 10 times without a miss.

- Repeat, seeing how many times in 1 minute.

- "Cradle" the ball between your legs 20 times without a miss.

- Perform an overhead drop and behind-the-back catch 5 times without missing.

- Repeat, seeing how many catches in 1 minute (misses don't count).

Basketball Skills
Station 3, Passing

- Bounce the ball between your legs and catch it behind your back, 5 times without missing; repeat 10 times.

- Perform a chest pass, hitting a target 15 feet away, 5 times without missing.

- Repeat using a bounce pass.

- Perform a bounce pass with a partner, 10 feet away, hitting a coin placed midway between, 7 to 10 times.

- Perform 10 passes from one side of a wall target, and catch the rebound on the opposite side, 5 to 10 times.

Basketball Skills
Station 4, Shooting

- Make 5 out of 7 shots from close range demonstrating good form.

- Make 3 out of 5 shots with your dominate hand, at a 45-degree angle from the basket, on either side.

- Repeat using the nondominate hand and changing sides.

- Bounce the ball off the backboard, rebound it quickly, and shoot immediately. Try making it 4 out of 7 times.

- Using the "Around the World" marks for shooting, see how many baskets you can make.

- Make 3 out of 6 right-handed lay-ins.

- Make 3 out of 6 left-handed lay-ins.

STATION BASKETBALL (4-8)

Focus: Refinement of basketball skills

Equipment: Basketballs, task cards, cone, jump ropes, marker

Description:

A station activity emphasizing specific basketball skills in a fast-moving activity designed to allow for success by all students.

Procedure:

Develop station task cards for each activity and post at each activity area. Place appropriate number of basketballs and a jump rope for each person at each station. Divide students into groups and assign to a station.

1. When the start signal is given, all students begin performing the task listed for that station.
2. After working at the station tasks for a predetermined time, the signal for all students to begin jumping rope is given.
3. Students jump rope for 1 to 3 minutes, then rotate clockwise to the next station.
4. Continue until all stations are completed. Conclude with 3 minutes of jump rope followed by a 1-minute walk.

Organization:

Have the students work individually. After they have completed the assigned task, they jump rope and rotate on their own.

Basketball Skill Challenge Beginning Level

Can You?

Toss the ball quickly around body 10 times without missing.

Stand and bounce the ball between legs and catch it behind yourself 5 out of 7 times.

Figure-8 the ball around legs 10 consecutive times.

Dribble the ball around body 10 times while standing in place.

Standing in place, bounce the ball from behind, through legs, and start dribbling in front. (Dribble 5 times for completion of task. Repeat the entire task 5 times.)

Standing with feet apart, dribble the ball in a figure-8 around legs 5 times.

Standing in place, eyes closed, dribble the ball with one hand 10 times without missing.

Toss ball in air, head high, clap hands behind back, catch ball 10 consecutive times.

Bounce ball off backboard, catch it, and quickly make a shot, 3 out of 5 times.

Standing with feet apart, hold ball between legs with right hand in front and left hand in back. Without letting the ball touch the ground, switch places with the hand (left goes to front and right goes to back) 5 times.

While performing a wall sit, chest pass with a partner for 30 seconds.

Completion Date: _____

Teacher Signature: _____

Basketball Skill Challenge
Intermediate Level

Can You?

Alternating hands, dribble the ball 5 times under the left leg and 5 times under the right leg.

Standing with feet apart, do a reverse figure-8 dribble 10 times without missing.

Bounce pass to a target 15 feet away 10 times without missing.

With eyes closed, dribble the ball around body 5 times.

While walking, bounce the ball from behind, through legs, and start dribbling in front. (Dribble 5 times for completion of task.)

Chest pass to a target 15 feet away 10 times without missing.

Standing in place, eyes closed, dribble the ball, alternating hand 20 times without missing.

With a partner, slide down 30 feet and back, chest passing the ball the entire time.

Standing with feet apart, dribble ball around and through your legs with dominate hand 5 times.

From a push-up position, dribble ball under body using the dominate hand, 30 seconds without missing. Using the nondominate hand for 30 seconds.

Completion Date: _____

Teacher Signature: _____

Basketball Skill Challenge
Advanced Level

Can You?

Make 5 out of 7 shots from in front of the basket with good form.

Perform a 3-man weave with two other people the length of the play area with no mistakes.

With a partner 10 feet away, bounce pass, hitting a coin placed midway between, 7 out of 10 times.

With eyes closed, begin walking forward approximately 30 feet, dribbling the ball without missing.

Make 5 bounce passes from one side of a wall target and catch the rebound on the opposite side.

Make 5 out of 7 shots from the left side of the basket with good form.

Hit a target 15 feet away from a sitting position using a chest pass.

With a partner, slide down 30 feet and back, bounce passing the ball the entire time.

Standing with feet apart, dribble ball around and through your legs with non-dominate hand 5 times.

While performing a wall sit, catch bounce passes from a partner for 30 seconds. (Keep back against wall, legs at 90 degrees, and chest pass the ball back.)

Completion Date: _____

Teacher Signature: _____

Floor Hockey Skills and Fitness

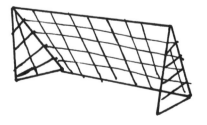

FLOOR HOCKEY WEAVE (2-4)

Focus: Speed and agility while developing hockey skill

Equipment: 2 hockey sticks, 1 puck, and 4 cones per group

Description:

Students are arranged in groups of four with two from each group at each end of the facility. Students dribble the puck around a series of cones, circle the last cone in the series, and pass the puck to the next person on their team.

Procedure:

Arrange students with two team members on each end of the facility. The first person at each end holds a hockey stick.

1. On the go signal, the first student on each team dribbles the puck through a series of cones. When coming to the last cone, they circle the cone and pass the puck to the next team member.
2. After passing, the person runs to the end line.
3. Upon receiving the puck, the person dribbles straight out to the center, circles the first cone, and continues through the series of cones, handing off the puck and stick to the next person.
4. Continue the rotation until all players have had two chances and are in their starting positions.

Organization:

Shorten the length of the activity area for younger or less-skilled students.

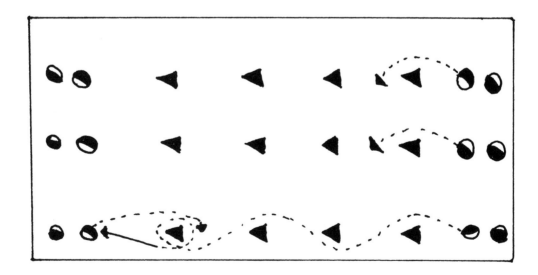

FLOOR HOCKEY RELAY (3-5)

Focus: Stick/puck control and agility

Equipment: 1 puck and stick per group

Description:

Students are in pairs, each with one floor hockey stick and puck. Students are lined up on one side of the facility in relay formation with one hockey stick per group and one puck per group on the opposite side. Students run to one side and dribble the puck back.

Procedure:

Line up students in relay formation facing their puck located on the opposite side of the facility.

1. On the start signal, the first team member runs out to the puck, carrying the hockey stick, and dribbles it back to the waiting partner.
2. Upon receiving the puck, the second partner dribbles the puck to the opposite side of the facility and runs back to hand the stick to his or her partner.
3. Continue the rotation for several minutes, encouraging speed and control.

Modification:

1. Put a cone marker at the halfway point. Have the students circle the cone one time when dribbling the puck.
2. Have students pass the puck to their partner and/or a cone marker when finishing their dribble.
3. Have the waiting partner jump rope or juggle.

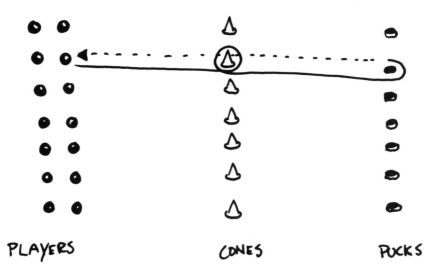

PLAYERS   CONES   PUCKS

FLOOR HOCKEY EMPHASIS STATIONS (3-7)

Focus: Challenging activities for each skill component

Equipment: Sticks, pucks, cone markers, student cards

Description:

Students are divided into four groups and assigned to a specific emphasis station. Students work individually or in groups to accomplish the assigned tasks.

Procedure:

1. Assign students to emphasis stations.
2. Students spend 10 minutes at each station, moving from the beginning task to the ending task.
3. After students complete a station, you may check it off on individual student cards.

Modification:

1. For younger students, design emphasis stations to include basic skills using striking and moving.
2. Create additional challenges for students who progress through the stations.
3. Create lower-level challenges to allow all students to experience success.

Floor Hockey Skills
Station 1, Puck Control

- Using a "half" hockey stick (cut a stick to half the regular length), continuously move the puck in a figure-eight rotation between your legs for 30 seconds while remaining stationary.

- Using a "half" hockey stick, while sitting in a chair move a puck in a figure-eight rotation around cones placed on the floor in front of you for 30 seconds.

- Keep control of the puck while moving through a series of cones. While moving forward. While moving backward.

- Quickly move the puck through a series of cones making a complete circle around each cone. While moving forward. While moving backward.

© 1994 by Parker Publishing Company

Floor Hockey Skills
Station 2, Passing

- Pass to a target or stationary partner 15 feet away. 8 times out of 10. 10 times out of 10.

- Repeat the above task while moving forward.

- Repeat the above task while moving laterally.

- While stationary pass to a partner 15 feet away, using a forehand pass. A backhand pass. 8 times out of 10. 10 times out of 10.

- Repeat the above task while moving.

- While moving circle a cone and immediately pass to a partner 15 feet away. 5 times out of 10. 8 times out of 10.

Floor Hockey Skills
Station 3, Shooting

- While stationary make 5 shots from 10 feet away using good form.

- Repeat the above while moving forward. Then try moving laterally.

- Make 5 forehand and 5 backhand shots from 15 feet while stationary. While moving forward. 5 times out of 10. 8 times out of 10.

- While stationary, receive a pass and immediately shoot from 15 feet. While moving forward. While moving laterally. 5 times out of 10. 8 times out of 10.

- Make a shot from different angles repeating the above activities.

Floor Hockey Skills
Station 4, Defense

- While standing in the goal box, block 5 shots made from 15 feet away. 5 times out of 10. 8 times out of 10.

- Repeat the above with shots made from different angles.

- With a partner, "steal" the puck while both of you are moving.

- Standing in a 10-foot circle, play one-on-one with your partner. A point is scored by a person moving the puck out of the circle and trapping it within 1 foot.

- "Intercept" a pass and immediately begin to move the puck forward.

FLOOR HOCKEY SKILLS CHALLENGE (3-7)

Focus: Floor hockey skills

Equipment: Floor hockey sticks, pucks, cone markers, challenge sheets

Description:

A variety of challenges to motivate students and provide them with alternative methods to practice both traditional and nontraditional activities related to floor hockey.

Procedure:

Design individual student challenge sheets and arrange the facility so that students may begin working on each challenge task.

1. Hand out the challenge sheets to each student. All students should begin with the lowest level challenges and progress through each task. This provides for review and challenge.
2. Demonstrate any activities that may not be familiar to the students.
3. Have the students choose which challenge to begin with and let them go to work.
4. As students accomplish a task, they should bring their task sheet to you for approval.
5. Once students have worked through the first level, give them the second level, etc.
6. Provide some type of rewards and reinforcement for completion of each level.

MODIFICATION:

If students are unable to complete any activity within an appropriate time, modify the activity as needed. If a modification is provided, make a note on the challenge sheet and encourage continued work on the original task.

Floor Hockey Skill Challenge
Beginning Level

CAN YOU?

Dribble the puck through 4 cones 3 feet apart in 15 seconds or less.

Pass accurately to a partner 10 feet away. 8 times out of 10. 10 times out of 10.

Stand with feet apart and move the puck around and through your legs. 8 times without a miss. 10 times without a miss.

As a goalie, block 8 shots out of 10 taken from 15 feet away. How about 10 out of 10.

Dribble the puck through a series of 3 cones and pass to a partner moving 10 feet to your side.

Completion Date: _____

Teacher Signature: _____

Floor Hockey Skill Challenge
Intermediate Level

CAN YOU?

Make 8 out of 10 shots on goal from 15 feet away while moving laterally. How about 10 out of 10.

Pass accurately to a partner 10 feet away while both of you are moving.

As a goalie, block 8 out of 10 shots attempted from 15 feet away. How about 10 out of 10.

Move, with a partner, down the floor passing a puck back and forth. Keep 10 feet apart.

Receive a pass from your partner, dribble around him or her, return to your spot, and pass.

Completion Date: _____

Teacher Signature: _____

Floor Hockey Skill Challenge
Advanced Level

CAN YOU?

As a goalie, block 8 of 10 shots made on goal by two opponents, passing and faking.

Standing with a partner in a 10-foot circle, try to dribble the puck out of the circle and stop it within 5 feet of the edge.

Dribble the puck through a series of 4 cones placed 3 feet apart in 10 seconds.

Make 8 of 10 shots on goal from 15 feet while moving forward.

Standing with feet apart, move the puck around and through your legs 10 times without a miss.

Completion Date: _____

Teacher Signature: _____

RUN AND GUN (4-6)

Focus: Dribbling and shooting skills, cardiovascular fitness

Equipment: Pucks, sticks, goals (cones or mats)

Description:

Students dribble a puck and attempt to shoot goals from various locations throughout the facility. Six goals are positioned in the facility. After a student attempts one shot, he or she will run to the next location, dribble, shoot, and run to the next location.

Procedure:

Set up six goals at different locations in the facility (use cones or mats placed on end if necessary). Place one hockey stick and several pucks at each goal.

1. On the go signal, the first student in each line takes a stick, runs to the puck, dribbles around a cone, and takes a shot.
2. After taking the shot, they return the stick to the line, run one lap, and stop at the next goal.
3. Repeat this activity until all students have returned to their starting line.

Modification:

1. Use whiffle balls instead of floor hockey pucks for faster action.
2. Have students go out in groups of two to pass the puck between them prior to one taking the shot.
3. Add a goalie for advanced students.

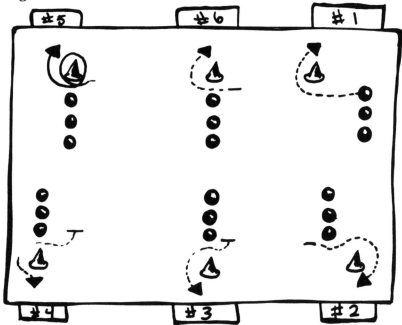

Football Skills and Fitness

HANDOFF (K-2)

Focus: Agility, movement skills, and cooperation

Equipment: Footballs (1 for each group of 2)

Description:

A fast-moving activity designed to use the student's interest in football to enhance movement and cooperation skills. One partner runs around the facility carrying a football and dodging others. When given the signal, they handoff to their partner.

Procedure:

Have each student take a partner and find an open space within set boundaries. Give each group a football. (Use any ball if there are not enough footballs.)

1. When the go signal is given, the partner with the ball begins to run around the facility (carrying the ball in the correct manner). The partner is standing in place or doing jumping jacks.
2. The stop signal is given after approximately 15 seconds. At that time the runner stops and holds the ball out for a handoff—end of the ball pointing to the side.
3. After all students have stopped, call out "Handoff."
4. Hearing the signal "Handoff," the partner not holding the ball runs to his or her partner, takes the ball, and begins to run.
5. Repeat this rotation.

Use and Modification:

1. This activity can be used as a warm-up for older students or as a learning activity for younger students.
2. If students are skilled in passing or centering, have them practice those skills instead of the handoff. Get within five yards before passing and make sure nobody is in the way.

FLAG TAG (K-2)

Focus: Refining movement, agility

Equipment: Flags, belts

Description:

A fast-moving tag game in which no student is eliminated and all can be successful.

Procedure:

Give each student a flag belt and two flags. After students have their belts on, have them get into a scatter formation. Explain that they must stay within the boundaries. If they bump into another person, they must *both* stop and raise their hands until told to go again (5 seconds).

1. On the go signal, all students begin to run around the facility.
2. Students try to pull one flag off another person's belt.
3. If a student's flag is pulled, he or she must stop, hold it in the air, count to 15, then put the flag back on the belt again.
4. Keep a close watch to make sure students stop when their flag is pulled and that they do not "guard" their flag with their hands.

Modification:

Change locomoter movements during the activity; e.g., skip, gallop, etc.

FOOTBALL SKILLS CHALLENGES (K–2)

Focus: Refinement of skills

Equipment: Nerf™ footballs, instructor check list

Description:

A variety of skill challenges designed to motivate students and provide alternative methods to practice the skills. Both traditional and nontraditional activities are utilized to provide success opportunities for students at all ability levels.

Procedure:

1. Provide each student with a ball.
2. Arrange students for a quick check off. (See "Organization" below.)
3. Demonstrate the activities as necessary.
4. Allow students time to practice challenges.
5. Begin checking off students who can complete each challenge.
6. After the first level has been completed, move student to next level.
7. Provide certificates after each level for completion and positive reinforcement.

Organization:

1. If you have the students arranged in typical squad formation (alphabetically), this will allow you to watch more of them at one time and check off the skills completed.
2. When checking off the skills, it is sometimes easier to mark only the student who **cannot** complete the challenge.
3. If you find the challenges are too difficult (more than 30% of the class not able to complete), modify to a lower level for greater success.

Football Skill Challenge
Beginning Level

CAN YOU?

Toss and catch the football to yourself 3 times without missing.

Toss and catch the football with a partner 3 times without missing. (Each person tosses 3 times and catches 3 times.)

Lay the ball on the ground and kick it from a stationary position. (The kick should be made in the middle of the ball.)

Hike the ball to your partner who is standing approximately 5 feet away.

Completion Date: _____

Teacher Signature: _____

Football Skill Challenge
Intermediate Level

CAN YOU?

Toss and catch the football to yourself 6 times without missing.

Toss and catch the football with a partner 6 out of 10 times without missing. (Each person tosses 5 times and catches 5 times.)

Kick the ball from a football tee from a stationary position.

Hike the ball to your partner who is standing approximately 7 to 10 feet away.

Catch a hike from your partner who is standing 7 to 10 feet away.

Completion Date: _____

Teacher Signature: _____

Football Skill Challenge
Advanced Level

CAN YOU?

Toss and catch the football to yourself 6 times without missing.

Toss and catch the football with a partner 6 out of 10 times without missing while walking forward.

Kick the ball from a football tee using a 3-step approach.

Hike the ball to a target 5 feet away and hit it 3 out of 6 times.

Catch a pass from your partner while running 5 to 10 feet in front of him or her.

Completion Date: _____

Teacher Signature: _____

Flag Football Fitness (3–5)

Focus: Agility skills, increasing aerobic capacity

Equipment: Flags, belts

Description:

A fast-moving activity with students trying to capture as many flags as possible within a designated time period.

Procedure:

Scatter two teams on their respective sides of the field.

1. Mark boundaries for the play area.
2. Divide students into teams and give out respective flags. Have students move to their side of the field.
3. On the "start" signal, the two teams begin chasing each other, trying to steal as many of the opponent's flags as possible until time is called or one team loses all its flags.

Rules:

1. No flags may be tucked in pants or pockets.
2. Once both flags are stolen, the student is eliminated and may not steal anyone else's flag.
3. Emphasize safety precautions for stealing flags and dodging.
4. Once eliminated, the student leaves the field carefully and stands on a sideline until a new game begins.

Modifications:

1. *No Team Steal:* Everyone is stealing from everyone else, with no team designations. This modification makes the activity move a little slower since there are more flags to steal.
2. *Exchange Steal:* Students may exchange flags they have stolen for one of their own to get back in the game. Have an "exchange store" set up so when a student comes to exchange one color flag for another, someone can monitor it.
3. *One on One:* Instead of the entire class, play one-on-one steal.

Use:

This is a fast-moving activity, so moving into the modifications is usually necessary. It is also a good opening activity for a short duration time frame.

Football Skills Challenges (3-8)

Focus: Refine football skills

Equipment: Footballs, Nerf™ balls, hoops, challenge sheets

Description:

A variety of challenges to motivate students and provide them with alternative methods to practice both traditional and nontraditional skills.

Procedure:

Design the individual challenge sheets and arrange the facility so that students may begin to move through the assigned tasks.

1. Provide students with challenge sheets beginning with the first level and demonstrate any activities the students may not be familiar performing.
2. Let students practice the activities. When they are ready to be challenged, have them bring their sheets to you to sign off.
3. Once students have worked through the first level, give them the second level, etc.
4. Provide some type of reward and reinforcement for completion of each level.

Modification:

If you find students are unable to complete any activity within an appropriate time frame, modify the activity.

Football Skills Challenge
Beginning Level

CAN YOU?

- With a partner 15 yards apart, stand, pass, and catch 5 out of 7 times without missing.

- With a partner 10 yards away, successfully hike to partner so he or she can catch it 5 out of 7 times.

- Place kick the ball so it covers a distance of 20 yards, going relatively straight 3 out of 6 times.

- Punt the ball so it covers a distance of 20 yards, going relatively straight 3 out of 6 times.

- Toss a ball high in the air, make a complete turn, and catch the ball 3 out of 6 times.

- Pass a ball at a $3' \times 3'$ target 15 yards away using proper form. Hit the target 6 out of 10 times.

- Center a ball at a $3' \times 3'$ target 5 yards away. Hit the target 6 out of 10 times.

Completion Date: _____

Teacher Signature: _____

Football Skills Challenge
Intermediate Level

CAN YOU?

- Pass a ball to your partner while he or she is moving in front of you 15 yards away.

- Catch a ball thrown to you while you are running 15 yards in front of the passer.

- Punt the ball in the air so it has a hang time of 2 to 4 seconds.

- Hand off the ball to your partner as he or she runs past you 3 out of 5 times.

- Lateral pass the ball to your partner while he or she runs past you 3 yards on your left side.

- Lateral pass the ball to your partner while he or she runs past you 3 yards on your right side.

- Kick the ball towards a target 15 yards away so it lands within the width of the goal post. (Place cones at the width of the goal post.)

Completion Date: _____

Teacher Signature: _____

Football Skills Challenge
Advanced Level

CAN YOU?

- Punt the ball in the air so it has a hang time of 6 or more seconds. (The ball should go relatively straight.)

- Pass the ball through a slowly moving suspended 36″ hoop 10 yards away.

- Center the ball through a suspended 36″ hoop (1 foot off the ground) 5 yards away.

- Center the ball to your partner, run forward 20 yards, and catch a pass 3 out of 6 times.

- Kick the ball toward a target 20 yards away so it lands within the width of the goal post. (Set cones at the width of the goal post.)

- Lateral the ball back and forth with a partner 5 to 10 feet away while running forward for 15 yards.

Completion Date: _____

Teacher Signature: _____

Football Emphasis Stations (3–8)

Focus: Variety of challenging activities for each skill component

Equipment: Footballs, flags, Nerf™ footballs, flying discs, cone markers, student cards

Description:

Students are divided into four groups and assigned to a specific emphasis station. Students work individually or in groups to accomplish the assigned task.

Procedure:

1. Assign students to emphasis stations.
2. Students spend 10 minutes at each station moving from the beginning task to the ending task.
3. After completing a station, you may check it off on individual student cards.

Modification:

1. For younger students, design emphasis stations to include basic skills using a football to accomplish theme tasks of throwing, receiving, striking, and moving.
2. Create additional challenges for students who progress through the station. In addition, lower-level challenges should be made available in order to allow all students to experience success.

Football Skills
Station 1, Passing/Catching

- Standing 20 feet from a partner, run back 5 steps, stop, and throw the ball to partner who is stationary.

- Standing 20 feet from a partner, run back 5 steps, stop, and throw the ball to partner who is running away.

- Standing 20 feet from a partner, run towards partner and laterally pass the ball while partner is stationary.

- Stand 20 feet away from partner. On signal, both run towards each other and laterally pass the ball.

- Switch positions so partner completes the above tasks as the passer.

Football Skills
Station 2, Passing/Catching

- Using a flying disc, throw and catch to a partner, 20 feet away, accurately 10 times.

- Running a regular pass pattern, repeat the above activity 5 times.

© 1994 by Parker Publishing Company

- Have a partner run 5 different patterns, approximately 20 yards in length, and successfully throw the ball for each pattern. Partner should be able to catch the ball 4 out of 7 times.

- Stand with a partner at one end of the field. See how many throws and catches it takes to get to the other end of the field.

Football Skills
Station 3, Kicking/Punting

- Starting at one end of the field, see how many punts it takes to get to the other end of the field. The ball must be punted from where it lands.

- Standing in the center of the field, punt a ball to either side.

- Place kick a ball successfully 20, 25, and 30 yards.

- Place kick a field goal from the goal line, 5 yards back, and 10 yards back successfully 3 out of 5 times.

Football Skills
Station 4, Centering/Running

- Center the ball to a partner 5 yards behind, run a short pass pattern, and catch the pass from partner.

- Repeat, changing the distance to 10 yards.

- Run a zigzag pattern around and through the cones. Set the course for 5 to 7 cones 1 to 2 yards apart.

- Set up an area 15 × 10 yards. One person is at one end and the other person is at the opposite end. Person "A" throws the ball to Person "B." "B" catches the ball and tries to run past "A's" goal line without getting the flag stolen. Try for 3 out of 6 "touchdowns."

- Switch roles and repeat.

Racquet Sports Skills and Fitness

RACQUET SPORTS CHALLENGES (K-2)

Focus: Basics of sports skills

Equipment: Balloons, sponge balls, racquet, instructor check list

Description:

A variety of skill challenges designed to motivate students and provide alternative methods to practice the skills. Both traditional and nontraditional activities are utilized to provide success opportunities for students at all ability levels.

Procedure:

1. Provide each student with necessary equipment.
2. Arrange students for a quick check off. (See "Organization" below.)
3. Demonstrate the activities as necessary.
4. Allow students time to practice challenges.
5. Begin checking off students who can complete each challenge.
6. After the first level has been completed, move student to next level.
7. Provide certificates after each level for completion and positive reinforcement.

Organization:

1. If you have the students arranged in typical squad formation (alphabetically), this will allow you to watch more of them at one time and check off the skills completed.
2. When checking off the skills, it is sometimes easier to mark only the student who **cannot** complete the challenge.
3. If you find the challenges are too difficult (more than 30% of the class not able to complete), modify to a lower level for greater success.

Racquet Sports Skill Challenge
Beginning Level

In a Standing Position:
CAN YOU?

Bat a balloon to yourself using one hand for 20 seconds without missing.

Bat a balloon from one hand to the other for 20 seconds without missing.

In a Sitting Position:
CAN YOU?

Bat a balloon to yourself for 15 seconds without missing.

Bat a balloon from one hand to the other for 10 seconds without missing.

Bat a balloon to a partner for 15 seconds without missing.

In a Kneeling Position:
CAN YOU?

Bat a balloon to yourself for 15 seconds without missing using one hand.

Bat a balloon from one hand to the other for 10 seconds without missing.

Bat a balloon back and forth with a partner for 15 seconds without missing.

Completion Date: _____

Teacher Signature: _____

© 1994 by Parker Publishing Company

Racquet Sports Skill Challenge
Intermediate Level

CAN YOU?

Using a lightweight plastic racquet or nylon racquet, bat a balloon 5 to 10 times without missing while standing in a 36″ hoop/circle.

Walk forward batting the balloon off the racquet for a distance of 10 feet without losing control.

Using a sponge ball, bat the ball off the racquet 3 times without missing while standing in a 36″ hoop/circle.

Using a sponge ball, bat the ball off the racquet while moving forward for a distance of 5 feet without losing control.

Using a sponge/rubber ball that bounces, bat it against a wall 2 times without missing. Let the ball bounce once before hitting it again.

Completion Date: _____

Teacher Signature: _____

Racquet Sports Skill Challenge
Advanced Level

CAN YOU?

Place a ball on your racquet and keep it from falling off for 15 to 30 seconds.

Place a ball on your racquet, walk forward for a distance of 15 feet, and keep it from falling off.

Bat a balloon back and forth with a partner for 45 seconds without missing while each is standing in a hoop. (The hoops should be touching each other so the distance is not too great.)

While walking forward, bat a balloon back and forth to a partner for a distance of 5 to 10 feet.

Hit a ball tossed to you by your partner 3 times.

Completion Date: _____

Teacher Signature: _____

HANDBALL TENNIS (2-5)

Focus: Movement skills

Equipment: Tennis balls, basic tennis strokes

Description:

Students participate in either one-on-one or doubles on a small court without using a racquet. This is an excellent activity to teach movement and body positioning in relation to any racquet sport.

Procedure:

Draw small-sized courts on the floor. Each court should be approximately 4 feet wide and 8 feet in length. Have students get partners, get one ball and move to a court.

1. Play begins just like any racquet sport game and continues with serves and volleys.
2. Scoring and rules should be followed as closely as possible.
3. After games are completed, have students rotate to other courts.

Organization:

Have students alternate playing singles and doubles. Make doubles courts a little larger than the singles courts.

TETHERBALL-RACQUETBALL (2-5)

Focus: Refining forehand and backhand skills, coordination

Equipment: Ball suspended on a pole, pickleball paddle

Description:

A whiffle ball or tennis ball is suspended from a tetherball pole. Students play a game of tetherball using their paddles instead of hands. This is a fast-moving game that requires use of both forehand and backhand skills and body positioning.

Procedure:

Have students take partners and assign them to a specific court. To begin play, one player holds the ball and hits it forward; the other player then hits it back. The object is to keep the ball from wrapping around the pole in the direction your opponent is hitting.

1. Players must stay on their side of the centerline.
2. Proper form must be used when hitting the ball.
3. After one game is completed, players rotate to another area and begin play.

Organization:

If you do not have enough courts for all students to be playing at one time, have those waiting participate in a relay using paddles and balls.

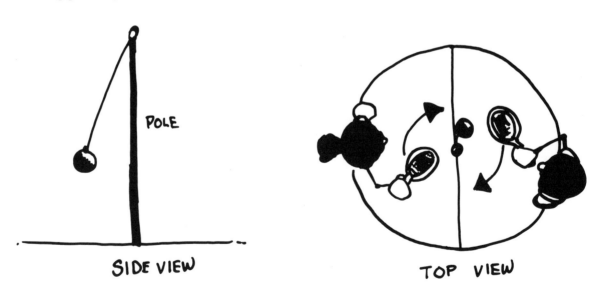

SIDE VIEW   POLE   TOP VIEW

RACQUET SPORTS CHALLENGES (3-8)

Focus: Racquet sports skills

Equipment: Various racquet sport equipment, challenge sheets

Description:

A variety of challenges designed to motivate students and provide them with alternative methods to practice both traditional and nontraditional skills.

Procedure:

The activities listed represent only a fraction of what is available and is included to help you get started. Use your inventory and imagination to develop your own challenges. Use tennis, badminton, pickleball, or racquetball equipment. You can also make your own with a coat hanger and nylons to be used with either balloons or foam balls.

1. Design individual challenge sheets.
2. Provide students with challenge sheets beginning with the first level. Demonstrate any activities with which students may not be familiar.
3. Have students practice the activities. When they are ready to be challenged, have them bring their sheets to you to sign.
4. Once students have worked through the first level, give them the second level, etc.
5. Provide some type of reward and reinforcement for completion of each level.

Motivation:

If students are unable to complete any activity within an appropriate time frame, modify the activity, note the modification on their card, and encourage continued work on the task.

Racquet Sports Skill Challenge
Beginning Level

CAN YOU?

While standing in a 36″ hoop/circle, hit the ball into the air, approximately head height, 10 times without missing.

While standing in a hoop, hit the ball on the ground, approximately waist height, 10 times without missing.

While standing in a hoop, hit the ball in the air, turn a full circle, let it bounce, and hit it again. 3 times out of 6. 5 times out of 6.

From 20 to 25 feet away, hit a ball tossed to you using a forehand stroke. 8 times out of 10. 10 times out of 10.

Repeat the task above using a backhand stroke.

Hit the ball off the wall allowing only one bounce before you hit it. 8 times out of 10. 10 times out of 10.

Completion Date: _____

Teacher Signature: _____

Equipment Used: _____

_____

Racquet Sports Skill Challenge Intermediate Level

CAN YOU?

Serve the ball over a taped line on the wall from 20 feet away (net height should be appropriate for the sport). 8 times out of 10. 10 times out of 10.

Using a forehand stroke, hit the ball into a 24″ × 24″ target taped on the wall. 8 times out of 10. 10 times out of 10.

Repeat the task above using a backhand stroke.

While standing in a 36″ hoop/circle, hit the ball into the air, approximately head height, alternating hits on each side of the racquet 15 times without missing.

With a partner, hit the ball back and forth without a miss. 8 times out of 10. 10 times out of 10.

Using the official serving line and net height, serve the ball successfully. 6 times out of 10. 8 times out of 10.

Completion Date: _____

Teacher Signature: _____

Equipment Used: _____

_____

Racquet Sports Skill Challenge
Advanced Level

CAN YOU?

Playing the ball off the wall, alternate forehand and backhand hits. 10 times consecutively. 15 times consecutively.

With a partner, hit the ball back and forth to each other 20 times (10 each) without a miss.

While sitting or kneeling, hit the ball in the air, head height. 8 consecutive times. 10 consecutive times.

Serve the ball to a partner on the opposite side of the net, within the boundaries of the specific sport. 8 times out of 10. 10 times out of 10.

Walk a 25′ taped line while hitting the ball on the ground in front of you.

While hitting the ball in the air, go from a standing position to a kneeling position and back to standing. 8 consecutive times. 10 consecutive times.

Completion Date: _____

Teacher Signature: _____

Equipment Used: _____

_____

TARGET RUN-AROUND (4-8)

Focus: Cardiovascular fitness, racquet sports skills

Equipment: Racquets, hula hoops, balls

Description:

Students are placed in groups of ten each in an area with a net (can be string or other net substitute) and a hula hoop. After hitting the ball, students run around the hoop and retrieve the ball. This is a fast-paced activity that students of all ages enjoy. Students in groups of ten or less can maintain constant movement.

Procedure:

On one side of the net, place a hula hoop approximately 15 feet from the net. Line up students, in groups of ten, on the other side of the net preparing to hit the ball towards the hoop. Give each student one ball. One racquet is enough for each group.

1. The first team member drop-hits the ball towards the hoop.
2. After hitting the ball, they must run around to retrieve the ball and get back in line before their next turn. (Keeping the hoop close to the net will demand an arching, thus keeping balls from being hit too hard and traveling long distances.)
3. As soon as the first player rounds the corner of the net, the next player in line hits.
4. Keep the activity moving until all players have had several opportunities.

Organization and Modification:

1. Caution must be exercised to ensure that no one hits the ball wildly.
2. Vary the location of the target after each team rotation so as to provide a challenge.
3. Award team points each time the target is hit.

RACQUET SPORTS EMPHASIS STATIONS (4–8)

Focus: Variety of challenging activities for each skill component

Equipment: Racquets, balls, cone markers, hula hoops, student cards

Description:

Students are divided into four groups and assigned to a specific emphasis station. Students work individually or in groups to accomplish the assigned tasks.

Procedure:

1. Assign students to emphasis stations.
2. Students spend 10 minutes at each station, moving from the beginning task to the ending task.
3. After completing a station, you may check it off on individual student cards.

Modification:

1. For younger students, design emphasis stations to include basic skills using paddles and balls, etc., to improve striking and movement skills.
2. Create additional challenges for students who progress through the stations. In addition, lower-level challenges should be made available in order to allow all students to experience success.

Racquet Sports
Station 1, Forehand

- Standing 10 feet from wall, hit the ball into the wall and return quickly, 15 times in a row, for 30 seconds without a miss.

- While sitting in a chair, hit the ball into the air for 30 seconds without a miss. For 60 seconds.

- Bounce a ball on your racket, run to a line 30 feet away, and return without losing control of the ball. Use the forehand grip. Repeat 10 times without stopping.

- Rally with a partner. After you hit the ball, turn a complete circle and be ready to return the ball.

Racquet Sports
Station 2, Backhand

- Standing 10 feet from the wall, hit the ball into the wall and return 15 times without a miss, continuously for 30 seconds. Continuously for 60 seconds.

- While sitting in a chair, bounce the ball, using a backhand grip, in the air 15 times without a miss. For 30 seconds. For 60 seconds.

- Bounce a ball on your racket, run to a line 30 feet away, and return. Repeat 10 times in a row.

- Drop-hit a backhand to your partner, turn a full circle, and return partner's hit.

Racquet Sports
Station 3, Serving

- Toss the ball into the air and hit it with your hand 10 times in a row. Use proper form.

- Serve 10 balls into each service court.

- Return 20 balls tossed or served into each service court.

- Place hula hoops in various positions within each service court. Hit each hoop 1 time for each 5 attempts. 3 out of 5 attempts.

TENNIS BASEBALL (5-8)

Focus: Tennis skills

Equipment: Racquets, balls, net

Description:

This activity combines racquet sports skills with the challenge of trying to get "hits" and "runs" as in baseball. Students are placed in teams each trying to score "runs" by hitting the ball into specific areas of the opposite court.

Procedure:

Divide students into two teams. One team is in the "field," the other is up at "bat." Each player in the field has a racquet and is "defending" a specific area of the court. The "batting" team is trying to hit a pitched ball into specific areas of the court. The "fielding" team is trying to return the hit ball.

1. The ball is pitched to a batter who hits the ball over the net.
2. A player on the fielding team tries to return the ball.
3. If the ball is returned, a rally begins between the batting player and those players on the fielding team.
4. If the ball is not returned, no more than one bounce is allowed. The batter runs to the appropriate base (determined by where the ball first bounces).
5. If the batting player fails to return a hit, he or she is out.
6. Score is kept as in baseball.
7. An entire team bats a round before going into the field.

Organization and Modification:

1. After each batter, the fielding team rotates positions in a clockwise direction.
2. The pitcher may either toss the ball to the batter or use a racquet. The pitch must be in an area where the batter may successfully hit it. There are no strike outs.

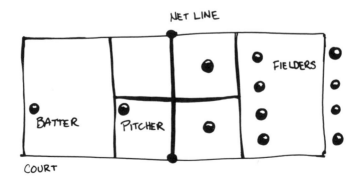

218

Rope-Skipping Skills and Fitness

ROPE-SKIPPING (1-8)

Focus: Basic skills

Equipment: Appropriate sized jump ropes

Description:

If students have previously learned the basic skills involved in rope skipping, start with a review before moving into the beginning level skills. *Note:* To reduce student frustration try working on individual progressions for short 10- to 15-minute periods of time for several weeks rather than the traditional unit of instruction.

Procedure:

Have each student select an appropriate sized rope. (While standing on the center of the rope and lifting the handles up, the handles should reach the arm pit area.) In teaching jump rope skills, have the students perform the steps first without turning the rope, then slowly with a rope turn. Do not spend a great deal of time on any one activity; this tends to cause frustration on the part of the student. After demonstrating and practicing without a rope, have students begin to work individually or in small groups moving through the progression. If frustration sets in with a student, have him or her move down the progression and then return to the activity that needs additional work.

Review Beginning-Level Skills:

- Basic **two-foot jump** (emphasis on proper body posture and jumping technique).
- Basic **one-foot hop.**
- Basic **jogging step.**
- Basic **steps changing speeds.**
- **Side Straddle** (10–15 times):

  1. Start with feet together.
  2. Jump rope landing in a lateral straddle position.
  3. Jump rope landing with feet together.

- **Front Straddle** (10–15 times):

  1. Jump to a Front Straddle position.
  2. Jump and reverse the position of feet.

- **X-Step** (10–15 times):

  1. Jump to a Side Straddle position.
  2. Jump to a position with feet crossed.

- ***Skier*** (10–15 times):

  1. Keeping feet close together, jump 6 inches to the side.
  2. Jump 6 inches to the other side.
  3. Keep shoulders facing straight ahead.

- ***Bell*** (10–15 times):

  1. Keeping feet close together, jump 6 inches forward.
  2. Jump 6 inches backward.

- ***Side Swing*** (10–15 times):

  1. Hold hands together at the side of the body.
  2. Turn the rope forward one time.
  3. Bring the hands to the other side of the body and swing the rope forward one time.

  Adding a Jump:

  1. After turning the rope one time at the side, return the rope to an open position and jump.
  2. Repeat on the other side of the body.

- ***Twister*** (10–15 times):

  1. Keeping feet together, jump while twisting hips and feet to one side.
  2. Repeat to the other side.

- ***Wounded Duck*** (10–15 times):

  1. Jump, landing with toes and knees pointing inward and touching.
  2. On the second jump, land with heels touching and knees pointing outward.

- ***Double Side Swing*** (10–15 times):

  Same as single Side Swing, but turn the rope at both sides prior to jumping.

Intermediate-Level Skills:

- ***Front Cross*** (10 times):

  1. Bring the rope overhead. Just before the jump, cross the arms in front. (*Hint:* Keep the hands at hip level, close to the body, and the rope handles held to the outside of the body.)
  2. As the rope clears under the feet, uncross the arms.

- ***Heel Toe*** (10 times):

  1. Hop on the right foot and touch the left heel forward.
  2. Hop again on the right foot and touch the left toe forward.
  3. Repeat using a left-foot hop and right-heel-and-toe touch.

- *Peek-a-Boo* (10 times):

  1. Hop on the right foot and touch the left toe to the floor about 12 inches to the side.
  2. On the second turn of the rope, do a basic two-foot jump.
  3. On the next turn, hop on the left foot and touch the right toe to the floor about 12 inches to the side.

- *Heel to Heel* (10 times):

  1. Hop on the left foot and touch the right heel to the floor in a forward position.
  2. Hop on the right foot and touch the left heel to the floor in a forward position.

- *Toe to Toe* (10 times):

  1. Hop on the left foot and touch the right toe to the floor behind.
  2. Hop on the right foot and touch the left toe to the floor behind.

- *Jogging Speed Step* (1 minute):

  1. Keep alternating steps on each turn of the rope.
  2. Count 1 every time the right foot touches the ground.
  3. Continue for one minute stepping as fast as possible.

- *Side-Swing Cross* (10 times):

  1. Complete Side Swing to the left side.
  2. Cross the left arm in front of the body to the right hip and jump.
  3. Repeat with a right Side Swing.

- *Can-Can Step* (10 times):

  1. Hop on the left foot, lift the right knee.
  2. Hop on the left foot and touch the right toe to the floor (don't put weight on the foot).
  3. Hop on the left foot and lift the right leg straight in front.
  4. Do a basic jump.
  5. Repeat using the opposite foot.

- *180-Degree Turnaround* (5 times):

  1. Perform a Side Swing to the left.
  2. As the rope turns, turn the body 180 degrees to the left (following the rope).
  3. Continue turning the rope, bringing it over the head in a back-turn direction.
  4. Jump rope backwards.

To continue the turn:
As the rope comes around, complete a Side Swing, follow the rope, and jump forward.

- *Double Under with Cross* (5 times):

  1. Perform a basic two-foot jump.
  2. As the rope begins its second turn, cross and turn the rope quickly (two times under with one jump).

Advanced-Level Skills:

- *Continuous Cross* (10 times):

  1. Perform a basic cross.
  2. Continue keeping the arms in a crossed position while turning the rope with the wrists.

- *Four-Point Touch* (10 each foot):

  1. Hop on the left foot and touch the right toe forward.
  2. On the second hop, touch the toe to the side.
  3. On the third hop, touch the toe in back.
  4. Repeat using the opposite foot.

- *Hopscotch* (10–15 each foot):

  1. Hop on the left foot and touch the right heel to the side.
  2. On the second hop, touch the right toe in front of the left foot.
  3. On the third hop, touch the right heel to the side.
  4. On the fourth hop, lift the right heel up and behind the left leg.
  5. Repeat using the opposite foot.

- *Leg Over* (5 each leg):

  1. Hop on the left leg and raise the right leg, foot slightly inward.
  2. Place the right hand under the right leg and continue to jump.
  3. When getting out of this position, bring both hands to the left and perform a Side Swing.

- *Leg Over with Cross* (5 each leg):

  1. Hop on left leg and raise the right leg, foot slightly inward.
  2. Place the left hand under the right leg and the right hand at the left hip, and continue to hop.
  3. When getting out of this position, bring the right leg down and perform a left Side Swing.

- *360-Degree Turn* (2 times):

  1. Begin with a left Side Swing.
  2. As the rope begins the Side Swing jump, make a complete 360-degree turn in the air. Land facing front and jump the rope prior to the landing.

- *Front-Back Cross* (5 times):

  1. Start in a left Side Swing position.
  2. Keep the right hand to the left side and bring the left hand behind to the right side.
  3. Jump the rope with hands in this position.

- *Back Cross* (5 times):

  1. Start in a basic forward two-foot jump.
  2. As the rope clears the feet, cross both arms behind the back.
  3. Using the wrists, continue turning the rope over the head and jump.

- *Double-Under Side-Swing Cross* (5 each side):

  1. Start in a basic forward two-foot jump.
  2. Perform a right Side Swing.
  3. Cross right arm in front to left hip.
  4. Perform a Double Under with arms across.
  5. Return to basic forward jump and repeat to the opposite side.

- *180-Degree Turn with Cross* (5 times):

  1. Perform a basic 180-degree turn.
  2. Cross the arms before landing and begin backward jumping.

Soccer Skills and Fitness

SOCCER SKILLS CHALLENGES (K-2)

Focus: Refinement of skills

Equipment: Playground balls (7 to $8\frac{1}{2}''$) or Nerf™ balls, instructor check list

Description:

A variety of skill challenges designed to motivate students and provide alternative methods to practice the skills. Both traditional and nontraditional activities are utilized to provide success opportunities for students at all ability levels.

Procedure:

1. Provide each student with a ball.
2. Arrange students for a quick check off. (See "Organization" below.)
3. Demonstrate the activities as necessary.
4. Allow students time to practice challenges.
5. Begin checking off students who can complete each challenge.
6. After the first level has been completed, move student to next level.
7. Provide certificates after each level for completion and positive reinforcement.

Organization:

1. If you have the students arranged in typical squad formation (alphabetically), this will allow you to watch more of them at one time and check off the skills completed.
2. When checking off the skills, it is sometimes easier to mark only the student who **cannot** complete the challenge.
3. If you find the challenges are too difficult (more than 30% of the class not able to complete), modify to a lower level for greater success.

Soccer Skills Challenge
Beginning Level

CAN YOU?

Drop the ball from head height, let it bounce a few times, and then trap it with your foot.

Kick a stationary ball with the inside of your foot in a forward direction.

Hold the ball over your head with two hands and throw it forward for a distance of 5 feet.

Lightly tap the ball with the inside of your foot, follow it, and trap it with the bottom of your foot before it stops rolling.

Completion Date: _____

Teacher Signature: _____

Soccer Skills Challenge
Intermediate Level

CAN YOU?

Drop the ball from head height, let it bounce a few times, and then trap it with your foot.

Using the inside of your foot, kick a ball that is slowly rolling towards you in a forward direction 3 out of 6 times.

Toss the ball slightly above your head and, as it descends, hit it with the top of your forehead.

Lightly tap the ball with the inside of your foot, follow it, and lightly tap it again (dribbling) before it stops rolling.

Standing 5 to 10 feet away from a wall, toss the ball to the wall. As it rebounds towards you, stop it with your torso or legs and trap it.

Completion Date: _____

Teacher Signature: _____

© 1994 by Parker Publishing Company

Soccer Skills Challenge
Advanced Level

CAN YOU?

Dribble the ball, with control, a distance of 10 to 15 feet. Then trap it with your foot to stop it.

Trap a ball rolling towards you, then kick it back to your partner using the inside of your foot.

Trap a ball that has been kicked to you from your partner.

Toss the ball slightly above and in front of your head, and head it 3 out of 5 tosses.

Head a ball tossed from your partner 3 out of 7 times.

Lightly kick a ball towards the wall, trap it, and kick it again. Do this sequence 3 times.

Completion Date: _____

Teacher Signature: _____

SOCCER FITNESS (3-8)

Focus: Cardiovascular fitness

Equipment: Soccer ball, cone markers

Description:

A station activity which incorporates fitness activities with skill development challenges related to basketball.

Procedure:

1. Divide students into groups equaling the number of stations you set (8 stations = 8 groups). It is recommended that you have at least 6 to 8 stations to minimize waiting.
2. Once the students are located at their station, give the signal to start the activity.
3. Once they have had their turn at the station, they are to run the perimeter of the facility and back to their *original station*. If time permits, they are to repeat the activity at that same station.
4. The students at the shooting station will usually dictate the time or rotation since it will take longer than the other skill stations. The students at the shooting stations *do not* have to perform the aerobic activity.
5. Rotate the students clockwise to the next station and begin.
6. Continue until all students have rotated all stations.

For Efficiency:

1. Impose a time limit on each station for each group to complete its task. Usually the students at the non-scoring stations will have a chance to complete the activity and run at least two times.
2. You might want to consider having challenges to see which group can complete the most rotations at the non-scoring stations to help keep them motivated.
3. A list of station suggestions appears below. Depending upon space, you may want more.

    Station 1: Direct shot toward goal, go through order 3 times. (Use for more than one station if space permits.)

    Station 2: Straight dribble down around cone and back with control.

    Station 3: Weave dribble between cones down and straight dribble back. When first students are on the way back, the second students begin.

    Station 4: Pass with partner and trap 15 feet apart.

    Station 5: Sprints between lines.

Station 6: With partner, move in a forward direction and pass the ball to one another. When done, pick it up and run back. When first group is done, the second group begins.

Station 7: Stationary heel-kick to partner 10 times.

Station 8: Moving heel-kick 15 feet.

Station 9: Punt the ball 5 times. (Have other group members retrieve ball for punter.)

Station 10: Chest trap ball from partner 10 times.

Station 11: Head the ball from partner 10 times.

4. If you do not have net goals to stop the ball, then position one student behind the goals to act as a retriever.

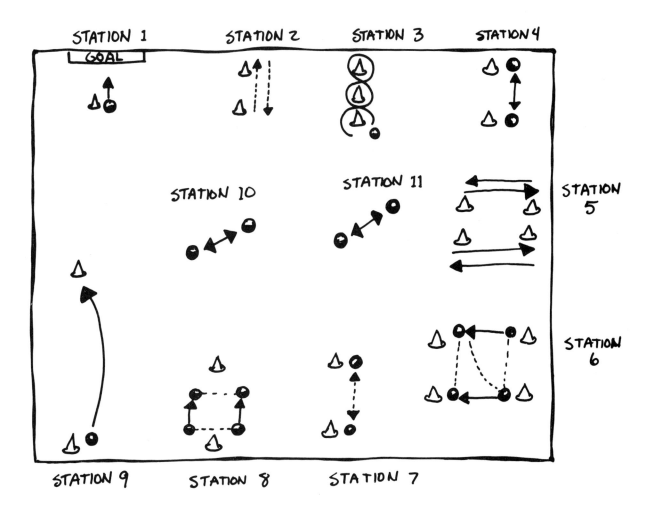

SOCCER EMPHASIS STATIONS (3–8)

Focus: Variety of challenging activities for each skill level

Equipment: Soccer balls, cone markers, student cards

Description:

Students are divided into three groups and assigned to a specific emphasis station. Students work individually or in groups to accomplish the assigned tasks before moving to the next level.

Procedure:

1. Assign students to emphasis stations.
2. Students spend 10 minutes at each station moving from the beginning level to the ending task.
3. After completing a station, you may check it off on individual student cards.

Modifications:

1. For the younger students, design emphasis stations to include basic skills using a soccer ball (or playground ball) to accomplish theme tasks of moving, striking, and receiving.
2. Create additional challenges for students who progress through the stations. In addition, lower-level challenges should be made available in order to allow all students to experience success.

Soccer Skills
Station 1, Dribbling/Trapping

- Using the inside/outside/toe/heel of your foot, pass a ball off a wall and make it come back to your partner. Keep alternating parts of your foot. Try 10 times in a row.

- Dribble a ball through a series of 5 cones, 3 feet apart, and return through the cones.

- Using a "foot bag" perform inside and outside kicks to yourself. Pass to a partner. Receive a pass.

- Standing 20 feet from a goal, take shots while standing still, moving forward, moving laterally.

Soccer Skills
Station 2, Ball Control

- While moving with a partner, dribble a ball and change directions when the signal is given by your partner. Pass the ball to your partner after 30 seconds and give the change directions.

- Standing within a 15′ × 15′ area, keep the ball away from your partner for 5 seconds, 10 seconds, longer.

- Bounce the ball off 3 different parts (foot to knee to chest) of your body.

- Using a "foot bag," bounce it off your knee, foot, and chest without losing control.

Soccer Skills
Station 3, Goal Keeping

- Stop 3 shots on goal made from 15 feet away by a partner who is moving forward, moving laterally.

- Use a punch, tip, and catch to stop a shot on goal and direct it back to a specific spot on the playing area.

- Staying within a 15′ × 15′ area, try taking a ball away from your partner within 10 seconds.

- While running beside your partner, try to "steal" the ball. Once you have control, begin to dribble and have your partner try to "steal" it from you. Keep within a 10-foot lane.

SOCCER SKILLS CHALLENGES (4-8)

Focus: Refine and enhance skills

Equipment: Soccer balls, challenge sheets

Description:

A variety of challenges to motivate students and provide them with alternative methods to practice both traditional and nontraditional skills.

Procedure:

The activities listed represent only a fraction of what is available. Use your inventory and imagination to develop your own challenges. A sample list of activities is included to help you get started.

1. Design the challenge sheets.
2. Provide students with challenge sheets beginning with the first level and demonstrate any activities with which the students may not be familiar.
3. Let students practice the activities. When they are ready to be challenged, have them bring their sheets to you to sign off.
4. Begin the activities and watch the fun!
5. Once students have worked through the first level, give them the second level, etc.
6. Provide some type of reward and reinforcement for completion of each level.

Organization:

If you find your students are unable to complete any activity within an appropriate time frame, modify the activity or number of completions as needed.

Soccer Skill Challenge
Beginning Level

CAN YOU?

From a stationary position, use an inside-the-foot kick, and kick ball straight to a partner, 10 feet away, 5 times, without partner having to move to trap the ball.

Trap the ball from your partner, who is performing the above skill, with a sole-foot trap, 5 times.

From a stationary position, make 4 out of 7 shots in the goal box (area) from a distance of 20 feet.

Dribble ball, alternating feet, 30 feet down and back.

Head a suspended ball 5 times in succession.

Punt the ball a distance of 15 yards so it passes between 2 cones, 10 feet apart.

Use an overhead throw-in, and hit a target 24″ × 24″ on the wall, from 15 feet out, 3 out of 6 times.

Completion Date: _____

Teacher Signature: _____

Soccer Skill Challenge
Intermediate Level

CAN YOU?

Pass ball against the wall, 15 feet away, making it come directly back to you 7 times consecutively.

Zigzag dribble down and back between 4 cones, set 4 feet apart. Can you complete the task in 1 minute or less? Record your actual time: _____.

Pass accurately to a partner 10 feet away while both are moving, 5 consecutive times. (Try to cover distance of at least 30 feet.)

Dribble the ball 15 feet, trap it, and immediately kick it backwards to a partner 10 feet behind you. Partner then begins dribbling past you and repeats the challenge. Repeat 3 times each for task completion.

Head 6 out of 10 tossed balls directly back to partner 10 to 15 feet away.

Knee the ball 3 times consecutively.

Trap the ball with your chest and pass it back to a partner 10 feet away.

Completion Date: _____

Teacher Signature: _____

Soccer Skill Challenge
Advanced Level

CAN YOU?

Toss ball in air, head it, knee it, and then catch it 6 out of 10 times.

Contact the ball with knee, then foot, 3 times in a row without ball hitting ground.

Punt ball 30 yards so that it passes between 2 cones set 6 feet apart, 3 out of 5 times.

Zigzag dribble down and back between 4 cones, set 4 feet apart, in less time than you did in the previous level.

_____ Previous time   _____ Current time

Defend the goal from a partner's free kick successfully 4 out of 7 times.

Completion Date: _____

Teacher Signature: _____

Softball Skills and Fitness

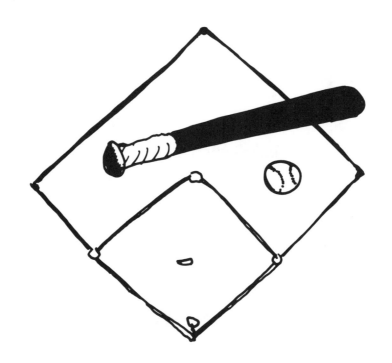

HIT AND RUN (K-2)

Focus: Basic batting and locomotor skills

Equipment: Plastic bats and balls, batting tee or cones

Description:

A low-organized activity allowing students to bat a ball off a tee and perform a fitness activity after each hit.

Procedure:

Arrange the facility so that there is a line of batting tees or cones on one side, each with one plastic ball and a plastic bat. Have students get in equal groups behind each tee.

1. The first player from each team stands up to the tee and, on signal, hits the ball.
2. After all balls have been hit, those students run to the other side, do five Pony Kicks, and run back to the line, picking up their ball on the way.
3. While those students are running, the others on their team do 5 Jumping Jacks, followed by 5 Pony Kicks.
4. After all balls have been returned and placed on the tee, the next person in line hits.
5. Repeat.

Organization and Modifications:

1. Make sure that all students stay back from the batter and that batters are cautioned not to run until the signal is given.
2. If you have more than three students per group, provide an alternative activity for those not involved. Then rotate groups.
3. After each hit, have all students run one lap and return.

SOFTBALL RELAY (2-4)

Focus: Refine skills, enhance fitness levels

Equipment: Softballs, bases, exercise cards

Description:

Within a game-type format, softball skills and fitness skills are integrated in a fast-paced approach. (This activity is a modification of "Kaos Ball" developed by Ron Liss, Garry Middle School, Spokane, WA.)

Procedure:

Divide students into teams of 5 or 6 each. The number of teams will depend on the playing area available. Bases/cones should be set 40 feet apart. Place an exercise task card at each base. Students "caught" at the base will perform that exercise.

1. A "batter" throws the ball into the outfield and begins to run the bases for his or her area.
2. Fielders get the ball as quickly as possible and throw it back to the catcher.
3. When the catcher receives the ball, he or she yells "stop."
4. If the runner is off base at the stop command, he or she must return to the base just vacated regardless of how far he or she is from it. The runner then performs the exercise listed for that base.

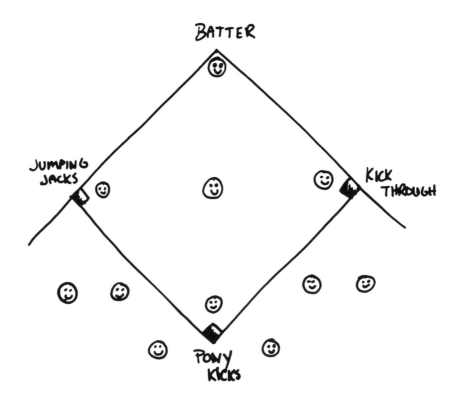

5. After all exercises have been completed, the next "batter" throws the ball.

6. There is no limit to the number of players who may be on one base at any time.

7. Continue until all players on the team have "batted." Then switch.

Organization and Sample Exercises:

1. Prepare the exercise task cards from posterboard and attach them to cones at each base. The activities selected should not require equipment or much space.

2. After students begin to understand the concept, add a pitcher. The pitcher will "pitch" the ball to the "batter" who must catch it and throw it to the field within 5 seconds.

3. Suggested sample exercises to use: push-ups (variations), crunches, v-sits, mountain climbers, bicycle, crab kick, heel slap/knee tap, and squat thrust.

AROUND-THE-WORLD SOFTBALL (3-6)

Focus: Total fitness

Equipment: Softball, bases, bat/tee

Description:

A fast-moving game involving all students.

Procedure:

Divide students into two equal teams. One team assumes positions in the outfield; the other team is "at bat." Using a batting tee (or pitching the ball), the first batter hits the ball and begins to run the bases as in a regular softball game. The fielding team responds as in a regular game. After the first batter is on base, the game begins to change.

1. All players on the batting team bat regardless of the number of outs.
2. There are no forced outs. Players must be put out by being touched or on a caught fly ball.
3. After a runner crosses home plate, he or she gets an automatic walk to first.
4. Runners do not have to run when a ball is hit.
5. There is no limit as to how many people may be on a base.
6. After the last person on the team has hit, all runners keep running the bases until the ball is placed on the tee or the catcher has the ball.

Organization:

Trying to keep score is almost impossible. This eliminates students from asking "who won" or "who is ahead."

SOFTBALL EMPHASIS STATIONS (3-8)

Focus: Variety of challenging activities for each skill component

Equipment: Softballs, bats, cone markers, Velcro™ glove, Foxtails™, ball on string, student cards

Description:

Students are divided into four groups and assigned to a specific emphasis station. Students work individually or in groups to accomplish the assigned task.

Procedure:

1. Assign students to emphasis stations.
2. Students spend 10 minutes at each station moving from the beginning task to the ending task.
3. After completing a station, you may check it off on individual student cards.

Modification:

1. For younger students, design emphasis stations to include basic skills using a softball to accomplish theme tasks of throwing, receiving, striking, and moving.
2. Create additional challenges for students who progress through the station. In addition, lower-level challenges should be made available in order to allow all students to experience success.

Softball Skills
Station 1, Catching

- Toss a ball in the air (3 to 4 feet), turn around, and catch it.

- With a partner standing on a bench holding a ball at head height, catch the ball when it is dropped. Try it with your hands on your hips before ball is dropped.

- Using Velcro™ gloves play Short Hop with your partner. (The ball bounces off the ground a short distance from you.)

- Facing a wall, throw a tennis ball into the wall, turn, and catch it over your shoulder 5 to 10 feet from the wall.

- Using a Foxtail™ thrown by a partner, catch it 5 times by each color segment.

Softball Skills
Station 2, Batting

- With a ball suspended from a pole, hit it 15 consecutive times.

- With a partner standing on a bench, hit a ball as it is dropped.

- Using a ball suspended on a long line, hit the ball as it is swung around by a partner. (Partner is kneeling while swinging the ball overhead.)

- Bunt a ball tossed by a partner to a specific target (directly in front, to the right side, to the left side).

Softball Skills
Station 3, Throwing

- Throw a ball through a suspended hula hoop 20 feet away. Try underhand. Try overhand.

- Throw a tennis ball into a wall 20 feet away, 20 times in 30 seconds.

- With a bucket suspended between two standards, toss (underhand) a ball into the bucket from 20 feet away 5 times. 10 times.

- Catch a tossed fly ball and immediately throw to a target 40 feet away 5 times. 10 times.

- Catch a grounder and immediately throw to a target 40 feet away 5 times. 10 times.

Softball Skills
Station 4, Running/Coordination

- Run around the bases, touching each base on the inside with your right foot.

- Play "pickle" with two others and successfully get to a base 3 times without being tagged.

- Do the Shuttle Run (running between two lines 30 feet apart) in 10.5 seconds.

- With a softball placed between your feet, kick it up and catch it. In front. To each side. In back.

SOFTBALL CHALLENGES (3-8)

Focus: Refine and enhance softball skills

Equipment: Softballs, batting tee, challenge sheets

Description:

A variety of challenges to motivate students and provide them with alternative methods to practice both traditional and nontraditional skills.

Procedure:

1. Divide students into groups according to the number of stations set up.
2. Provide students with challenge sheets beginning with the first level. Demonstrate any skills with which the students might not be familiar.
3. Let students practice the activities. When they are ready to be tested, have them bring their sheets to you for a sign-off.
4. Once students have worked through the first level, give them level 2, etc.
5. Provide some type of reward and reinforcement for completion of each level.

Organization and Modification:

1. The activities listed represent only a fraction of what is available. Use your inventory and imagination to develop different challenges.
2. If students are unable to complete any activity within an appropriate time frame, modify the activity to allow for success. However, note that a modification was made, indicating that the student still requires work in that skill area.

Softball Skill Challenge
Beginning Level

CAN YOU?

Toss a ball straight up and catch it 9 out of 10 times.

Toss the ball straight up, touch the floor, and catch it 9 out of 10 times.

Toss the ball straight up, sit down, and catch it 7 out of 10 times.

Pitch underhand and hit a 24″ × 24″ target taped on a wall 15 feet away 7 out of 10 times.

Toss a ball in the air and catch it with your non-dominate hand 8 out of 10 times.

Hit a suspended ball that is hanging still or off a tee 9 out of 10 times.

Completion Date: _____

Teacher Signature: _____

Softball Skill Challenge
Intermediate Level

CAN YOU?

Throw overhand to your partner 30 feet away so that he or she can catch it without moving, 7 out of 10 times.

Catch an overhand throw from your partner 30 feet away 7 out of 10 times.

Catch a ball tossed from 20 to 30 feet away to your non-dominate side 8 out of 10 times.

Hit 6 out of 10 "good" pitched balls.

Hit 8 out of 10 self-tossed balls.

Pitch underhand and hit a 24″ × 24″ target taped on a wall 30 feet away.

Catch a grounder tossed by a partner 20 feet away 9 out of 10 times.

Completion Date: _____

Teacher Signature: _____

Softball Skill Challenge
Advanced Level

CAN YOU?

Hit a self-tossed ball back to a partner 7 out of 10 times. (Your partner should not have to move more than one step.)

Hit 9 out of 10 "good" pitcher-tossed balls into fair territory.

Pitch underhand and hit a 24″ × 24″ target taped on a wall from 35 feet away 7 out of 10 times.

Catch 8 out of 10 throws from your partner, 40 feet away, when he or she throws in different directions; e.g., some to your right, some to your left, and some behind you.

Toss a ball straight up in the air, catch it, and immediately throw overhand to a partner 30 feet away 7 out of 10 times.

Catch a tossed grounder and immediately throw back to a partner 40 feet away 7 out of 10 times.

Completion Date: _____

Teacher Signature: _____

Volleyball Skills and Fitness

OVER-THE-LINE VOLLEY (K–2)

Focus: Volleyball skills, perceptual awareness

Equipment: Balloons, jump ropes

Description:

A low-organized partner activity. Partners stand facing each other with a jump rope lying on the floor between them. Each group has a balloon and attempts to keep it in the air between them.

Procedure:

Have students move randomly around the facility. When the stop signal is given, have students find a partner and stop. Have one partner get a jump rope and the other, a balloon.

1. Have the students place the jump rope on the ground between them.
2. Each partner stands 2 or 3 feet back from the rope. (Students with lower-ability levels can stand closer.)
3. Students begin hitting the balloon, with one or two hands, back and forth.
4. See who can keep the balloon going the longest.

Modifications:

1. Have students clap their hands 2 times after they pass the balloon.
2. Have students jump in the air 3 times after they pass the balloon.
3. After passing the balloon back and forth 5 times, have them run or skip around the facility until you say stop. Hearing stop, they find another partner; those holding the balloon find a partner without a balloon.

VOLLEYBALL SKILLS CHALLENGES (K-2)

Focus: Refinement of skills

Equipment: Beachballs, balloons, trainer volleyballs or regular volleyballs, instructor check list

Description:

A variety of skill challenges designed to motivate students and provide alternative methods to practice the skills. Both traditional and nontraditional activities are utilized to provide success opportunities for students at all ability levels.

Procedure:

1. Provide each student with a ball.
2. Arrange students for a quick check off. (See "Organization" below.)
3. Demonstrate the activities as necessary.
4. Allow students time to practice challenges.
5. Begin checking off students who can complete each challenge.
6. After the first level has been completed, move students to next level.
7. Provide certificates after each level for completion and positive reinforcement.

Organization:

1. If you have the students arranged in typical squad formation (alphabetically), this will allow you to watch more of them at one time and check off the skills completed.
2. When checking off the skills, it is sometimes easier to mark only the student who **cannot** complete the challenge.
3. If you find the challenges are too difficult (more than 30% of the class not able to complete), modify to a lower level for greater success.

Volleyball Skill Challenge
Beginning Level

CAN YOU?

Tap a balloon with your palm 5 times while standing in a hula hoop.

Toss your balloon up in the air with one hand and bat it forward with your other hand 3 times.

Clasp your hands together and hit your balloon in the air 3 times while standing in a hula hoop.

Hit a balloon back and forth to your partner with one hand 5 times. (Each person gets to hit the balloon 5 times.)

Completion Date: _____

Teacher Signature: _____

Volleyball Skill Challenge
Intermediate Level

CAN YOU?

Tap a beachball upward with your palms 5 times while standing in a hula hoop.

Toss your beachball up in the air with one hand and bat it forward with your other hand 5 times.

Clasp your hands together and hit your beachball in the air 3 times while standing in a hula hoop.

Gently toss your beachball up in the air and hit it with one hand to a partner 3 times.

Catch a hit beachball from your partner 3 times.

Using your hands, tap the beachball against a wall 3 times in a row without missing.

Completion Date: _____

Teacher Signature: _____

Volleyball Skill Challenge
Advanced Level

CAN YOU?

Tap a volleyball trainer upward with your palms 5 times while standing in a hula hoop.

Toss your volleyball trainer up in the air with one hand and bat it forward with your other hand 5 times.

Clasp your hands together and hit your volleyball trainer in the air 3 times while standing in a hula hoop.

Gently toss your volleyball trainer up in the air and hit it with one hand to a partner 3 times.

Catch a hit volleyball trainer from your partner 3 times.

Using your hands, tap the volleyball trainer against a wall 3 times in a row without missing.

Completion Date: _____

Teacher Signature: _____

VOLLEYBALL REACTION (2-8)

Focus: Movement skills, body positioning, reactions

Equipment: None

Description:

Students react to directions by moving and performing appropriate skills. This is an excellent warm-up as well as skill-building activity.

Procedure:

Spread students in a random formation facing the leader. Have each student assume a good "ready" position: feet shoulder width apart, knees slightly bent, hands and arms held in front.

1. The leader quickly calls out either forward, right, left, or back. At the same time, the commands of set, bump, or spike are given; e.g., forward/set, right/bump.
2. Students respond appropriately and return immediately to a ready position.
3. Continue for 3 to 4 minutes.

Modification:

The leader changes locations, having the students face that direction as well as respond to the movement/skill commands.

POWER BALLOON VOLLEYBALL (2-8)

Focus: Volleyball skills of setting, spiking, and bumping

Equipment: Balloons, folding mats

Description:

In groups of four, students participate in challenging activity while practicing volleyball skills. (This activity is a modification of "Mat Volleyball" presented by L.F. Turner at the N.W. Secondary P.E. Conference, 1989.)

Procedure:

Place opened 4 × 8 or 5 × 10 tumbling mats on end in areas of the gym which allow for students to move around without interfering with other games. Have students get partners and arrange themselves in groups of four at a mat. Give each group one inflated balloon.

1. When given the start signal, students begin to play a regular game of volleyball using the mat as a net.
2. When serving, move the service line up almost to the mat and allow a "help" to get the serve over the net.

JUMP AND TOUCH FOR FITNESS (4–8)

Focus: Jumping ability, blocking technique, coordination

Equipment: Volleyball net

Description:

Students make lines on opposite sides of the net facing a partner. During the drill, students will jump and attempt to touch fingertips with the person opposite them and rotate one position to the right.

Procedure:

Adjust the height of the net to an appropriate level for the age and skill level of the class. (Take one of the taller students and have him or her reach up as high as possible and place the net approximately 2 inches above that height.) Have the students line up on opposite sides of the net facing another person.

1. On the go signal, students begin jumping as high as possible, trying to touch the fingertips of the person opposite them. If they cannot jump high enough to touch, have them jump and reach as high as possible. Concentrate on proper blocking form—both hands up and square to the net.

2. After 4 jumps, everyone rotates one position to the right with the end persons moving around to the ends to the opposite sides. Take only 5 seconds to rotate.

3. Repeat until all students are back at their starting position.

Modifications:

1. Have two different groups based on size and skill. Have the smaller or less-skilled students work on a lower net, thus allowing for all students to experience success and benefit from the activity.

2. Continue for a set time period (3 to 4 minutes). See how many rotations students can make. Keep records and use this for a daily warm-up and challenge.

VOLLEYBALL EMPHASIS STATIONS (4-8)

Focus: Variety of challenging activities for each skill component

Equipment: Volleyballs, nets, wall targets, student cards

Description:

Students are divided into four groups and assigned to a specific emphasis station. Students work individually or in groups to accomplish the assigned task.

Procedure:

1. Assign students to emphasis stations.
2. Students spend 10 minutes at each station moving from the beginning task to the ending task.
3. After completing a station, you may check it off on individual student cards.

Modification:

1. For younger students, design emphasis stations to include basic skills using volleyballs, beachballs, volleyball trainers, or balloons to accomplish theme tasks of bumping, setting, serving, and moving.
2. Create additional challenges for students who progress through the stations. In addition, lower-level challenges should be made available in order to allow all students to experience success.
3. Use volleyball trainers and beachballs before moving to regular volleyballs.

Volleyball Skills
Station 1, Serving

- Perform an underhand serve over the net from 20 feet. From the regulation service line. 8 times out of 10.

- Repeat the above task using an overhand serve.

- Serve a ball into each quadrant of the receiving court using an underhand serve, 8 times out of 10. Using an overhand serve, 8 times out of 10.

- Serve a "floater" 5 times out of 10.

- Serve a "spinner" 5 times out of 10.

- Repeat the above, placing a serve in each quadrant of the receiving court.

Volleyball Skills
Station 2, Bump and Set

- How many times can you volley a ball above a taped line (8 feet) in 30 seconds? 10 times? 15 times? 20 times?

- With closed hands, bump a ball continuously against a wall for 20 seconds. Try with a partner and see who can go longer.

- Toss a ball into the net (or against the wall). Bump the rebound straight up 5 times out of 10. 8 times out of 10.

- From a position close to the net, set a ball to a partner so that the ball is close to the net and above it 5 times out of 10. 8 times out of 10.

- Repeat the above from the back court.

Volleyball Skills
Station 3, Spiking

- Without using a net, toss a ball into the air, jump up, and spike the ball down 5 times out of 10. 8 times out of 10.

- Repeat the above using a low net (5 feet).

- Without a net, jump up and spike a ball tossed by a partner 5 times out of 10. 8 times out of 10.

- Repeat the above task using a low net (5 feet).

- Repeat the second and fourth tasks using a regulation net (for your class and ability level).

Volleyball Skills
Station 4, Defense and Blocking

- Standing at the net, block (2-hand block) a partner's throw from across the low net (5 feet), 5 times out of 10. 8 times out of 10.

- Standing at the net, move laterally (minimum of 4 feet) and block a ball tossed by your partner from across the low net (5 feet) 5 times out of 10. 8 times out of 10.

- Repeat the first two tasks with a ball hit by your partner.

- Repeat the second and third tasks using a regulation net (for your class and ability level).

- Block a partner's spike from across a low net. A regulation net (for your class and ability level). 5 times out of 10. 8 times out of 10.

VOLLEYBALL SKILLS CHALLENGES (4-8)

Focus: Refine volleyball skills through creative challenges

Equipment: Volleyballs, trainers, beachballs, balloons, challenge sheets

Description:

A variety of challenges to motivate students and provide them with alternative methods to practice both specific volleyball skills and general movement activities related to volleyball.

Procedure:

Design individual student challenge sheets and arrange the facility so that students may begin working on each challenge task.

1. Hand out the challenge sheets to each student. All students should begin with the lowest level challenges and progress through each task.
2. Demonstrate any activities that may not be familiar to the students.
3. Have the students choose which challenge to begin with and let them go to work.
4. As students accomplish a task, they should bring their task sheet to you for approval.
5. Once students have worked through the first level, give them the second level, etc.
6. Provide some type of reward and reinforcement for completion of each level.

Modification:

If students are unable to complete any activity within an appropriate time, modify the activity as needed. If a modification is provided, make a note on their challenge sheet and encourage continued work on the original task.

Volleyball Skills Challenge
Beginning Level

CAN YOU?

Volley the ball above an 8-foot line on the wall 15 times in 30 seconds.

Volley a ball in the air to yourself for 30 seconds without missing.

Serve (underhand or overhand) from the service line (modified for your grade level) into the receiving court 8 out of 10 times.

With a low net, toss the ball into the air and spike it down 8 out of 10 times.

"Dig" a ball tossed low by your partner 8 out of 10 times.

Completion Date: _____

Teacher Signature: _____

Completed with: Trainer ____   Beachball ____   Volleyball ____

Volleyball Skills Challenge
Intermediate Level

CAN YOU?

"Bump" a ball against the wall above the 8-foot line from 5 feet away 8 out of 10 times.

Complete 8 out of 10 successful overhand serves from the regulation service line.

Set or bump a ball into the air, turn 90 degrees, and bump or set it again. Repeat this 5 times.

Toss a ball into the wall and rebound it with a bump or dig 8 out of 10 times.

Toss a ball into the air, spike it into the wall, and set the rebound.

Completion Date: _____

Teacher Signature: _____

Completed with: Trainer ____   Beachball ____   Volleyball ____

Volleyball Skills Challenge
Advanced Level

CAN YOU?

Bounce the ball on the floor, set it, let it bounce, and dig or set it 8 out of 10 times.

Set or bump the ball, make a 360-degree turn, and set it again 8 out of 10 times.

Toss the ball into the net and bump the rebound to a partner 8 out of 10 times.

Volley the ball against a wall 20 times in 30 seconds.

Spike a ball set by your partner over the net 8 out of 10 times.

Using an overhand serve, serve 10 out of 10 times into the receiving court.

Completion Date: _____

Teacher Signature: _____

Completed with: Trainer ____ Volleyball ____

4

Interdisciplinary Activities for Fitness

Enhancing the Knowledge Base

Educators throughout the country are constantly seeking ways to help students gain a greater understanding of the multitude of experiences and knowledge necessary to lead a healthy lifestyle. To lessen fragmentation, and enhance retention and use of knowledge, an interdisciplinary approach to teaching has become popular. By combining subject areas and reinforcing one subject in another class, you have an excellent method of enhancing student learning and retention.

An interdisciplinary approach to instruction can take several forms. One method is the block approach. In this method one individual is responsible for teaching two or three subjects to one group of students. In doing so the assignments many times will relate to each other and enhance all subjects. This approach is similar to the traditional elementary education setting where the students remain with one teacher for the entire day.

Another method of interdisciplinary instruction is to take concepts from a certain subject and apply them in a different setting. A good example would be using the laws of gravity. There are several methods to demonstrate Newton's Laws other than in the classroom.

A third method is to teach a concept or information in the physical education setting and enhance it in the classroom with follow-up information. Heart rate variation is an example. During physical education the instructor would have the students perform several tasks and record their heart rates during the task. Then, once they are back in the classroom, they could be lead through a guided discovery approach to decide how activity level influences heart rate. This approach could be accomplished cooperatively by the classroom teacher and physical education specialist or it could be done exclusively by either.

A final method of interdisciplinary instruction is to reinforce classroom concepts in combination with a physical education activity. An example from language arts would be the activity "Jumble Spell" found in this section. In this activity the students are performing certain physical tasks while learning how to spell and decipher coded words.

The student-centered activities presented in Section 4 provide an interactive and interdisciplinary approach designed to involve students at all ability levels in meaningful activities that are developmentally appropriate and fun.

MUSCULAR STRENGTH AND ENDURANCE (2-6)

Focus: Understanding concept of regular exercise and muscle development

Equipment: Student picture, exercises, muscles lists

Description:

An activity designed to provide students with practical and theoretical information for understanding the concept of regular exercise and major muscle groups.

Procedure:

1. In art class have the students draw a picture (outline) of themselves on a large sheet of butcher paper. Do not have them color it in. **Approximate time: one class period.**
2. Prepare a list of exercises that will use different muscle groups. This can be taped on the wall or given to each student.
3. Take the first exercise and have the students perform it. Once completed ask them what part of their body did it specifically work. They should respond "arms," "legs," "stomach," and so forth. If you are looking for a specific location, then you will need to probe further. For example, What part of our arm: upper, elbow, or wrist?
4. Once students have identified the area, have them write that exercise by that body part.
5. Have them perform exercises for all major body parts and label accordingly. Use the "Exercise Descriptions" in Section 2 to help identify major muscle groups.
6. You can repeat this activity another day by changing the exercises.

Modifications:

1. For the older students, begin a discussion of the muscles used in the exercises and have them label muscle locations as opposed to exercises.
2. Have the students generate a list of three to four exercises as a homework assignment for certain body parts.

Health-Related Fitness Components (4–8)

Focus: Health-related fitness concepts

Equipment: Overhead projector, pencils, worksheets

Description:

Several hands-on activities are provided that will present information on each of the four components of health-related fitness. Students are actively involved in each activity.

Procedure:

1. Conduct a class discussion of the definition of physical fitness and what physical fitness means to each student. Give students a few minutes to write on each of these ideas, then you can have small group discussions or one large group discussion. A good definition to go by is the one outlined by the President's Council on Physical Fitness and Sport: "The ability to carry out daily tasks with vigor and to engage in leisure time pursuits, and to meet the above average physical stresses encountered in emergency situations. **Approximate time: 10 minutes to write definition and what it means; 10 to 15 minutes to discuss as a large group.**

2. Ask students why it is important to keep physically fit. Have them write down their answers and then discuss. **Approximate time: 5 minutes to write answers; 5 to 10 minutes to discuss.**

3. Discuss the components of health-related physical fitness very quickly and in general terms. Place the following terms and definitions on the board or overhead projector so all students can see them. (This information will help with the next activity.) **Approximate time: 10 minutes.**

   a. *Muscular Strength:* How strong the muscles are.

   b. *Muscular Endurance:* How long the muscles can work.

   c. *Cardiovascular Endurance:* How much oxygen and nutrients the body can supply to working muscles.

   d. *Flexibility:* How far the muscles and tendons will stretch without harm to the individual.

   e. *Body Composition:* The relationship of lean body mass to fat.

4. Have students generate a list of 2 or 3 animals that tend to demonstrate the first four components. **Approximate time: 10 minutes.**

5. Divide the students into 4 to 6 groups (no more than 4 in a group), and have them come up with two activities or exercises that will enhance each of the first 4 fitness components. **Approximate time: 5 to 7 minutes.**

6. Using the same groups as above, or as a large class, have students generate a list of daily activities (non-fitness related) that require some level of physical fitness and what components each would primarily use. (For example: run-

ning to catch a bus = cardiovascular; moving furniture = strength and endurance; etc.) **Approximate time: 10 to 20 minutes, depending upon how in depth you want to carry the activity.**

7. As homework, assign the students to go through old magazines, cut out pictures that depict people who are physically fit, and bring them to class. Then have them put their pictures on the board and talk about the components of fitness that are depicted. For contrast, provide some pictures of people who may not be physically fit and discuss the differences. **Approximate time: 20 to 30 minutes.** (Leave the pictures up to reinforce the need for physical education in students' daily life.)

8. Review these components by making students aware of them when performing activities during the regular activity session.

Homework Assignment:

Have the students write 1-page reports using the following ideas for topics:

- Why it is important to be physically fit.
- Describe their three most favorite physical activities and include the components of physical fitness they incorporate.
- Visit with parents, siblings, and friends to find out what types of activities they participate in to stay physically fit and write a summary of findings.
- Visit with grandparents or a senior citizen to see how job and technology have changed the way people stay physically fit.
- Using the worksheets provided, participate in one or more of the following activities:

Exercise Journal: Keep a record for one week of your exercise habits. Record findings according to the questions on the worksheet.

Accomplishment Chart: Define 3 to 5 fitness goals to achieve in a period of 6 to 8 weeks. Use the attached worksheet to keep a record of progress.

3-Day Activity Record Worksheet: Similar to the Exercise Journal, this records the activities you participate in and how much time is spent to get an idea of your daily routine.

Activity Diary: This is similar to the 3-Day Activity Record Worksheet.

Activity Contract: Contract with your teacher for some physical activities for a specified period of time. Receive extra credit for completion.

EXERCISE JOURNAL

	List the exercise and duration each day	How did you feel?	Should you make changes?
Sunday			
Monday			
Tuesday			
Wednesday			
Thursday			
Friday			
Saturday			

ACCOMPLISHMENT CHART

In order to note progress towards meeting your goals, take time to write down your accomplishments on this chart and reward yourself for making them.

Date	Describe Accomplishments	Rewards (Personal or Material)

3-DAY ACTIVITY RECORD WORKSHEET

	Day 1 Activity	Time Spent	Day 2 Activity	Time Spent	Day 3 Activity	Time Spent
SLEEP						
GETTING UP UNTIL NOON MEAL						
NOON MEAL UNTIL EVENING MEAL						
EVENING MEAL UNTIL BEDTIME						
TOTALS						

ACTIVITY DIARY

Name _____

TIME	ACTIVITY	DURATION	LOCATION	PARTNERS	FEELINGS	
					BEFORE MY ACTIVITY	AFTER MY ACTIVITY
BEFORE BREAKFAST						
AFTER BREAKFAST						
BEFORE LUNCH						
AFTER LUNCH						
BEFORE DINNER						
AFTER DINNER						

ACTIVITY CONTRACT

1. I WILL DO:

Activities with friends _____

Activities alone _____

Activities indoors _____

Activities outdoors _____

2. EXERCISE IS A HEALTHY HABIT. I WILL:

Exercise   4   5   6   7   days each week.
(circle one)

Exercise   20   25   30   35   40   minutes each time.
(circle one)

KEEP INCREASING MY ACTIVITY
ONCE IT GETS EASY.
I WILL DO IT LONGER OR FASTER

3. I WILL TRY NEW ACTIVITIES AND WILL RE-TRY ACTIVITIES I MIGHT NOT HAVE LIKED AT FIRST.

4. I WILL REVIEW MY PROGRESS ON A REGULAR BASIS.

_____ Diet   _____ Strength

_____ Flexibility   _____ Alignment

_____ Endurance   _____ Body Composition

5. MY REWARD WILL BE A HEALTHY HAPPY ME!

**I WILL DO THESE ACTIVITIES FOR ME,
BECAUSE I'M WORTH IT!**

Student Signature: _____

Teacher Signature: _____

© 1994 by Parker Publishing Company

Performance-Related Fitness Components (4-8)

Focus: Performance-related fitness concepts

Equipment: Overhead projector, worksheets, pencils

Description:

Activities designed to help students to understand and differentiate between *performance*-related fitness and *health*-related fitness. Worksheets are provided for the activities.

Procedure:

1. Begin a discussion on performance-related fitness components. Performance-related components are skills related to, but not always necessary to maintain a healthy lifestyle. **Approximate time: 15 to 30 minutes.**

   a. *Agility:* The ability of a person to change direction of body position quickly, and control the movement of his or her entire body.
   b. *Balance:* The ability to maintain a desired position of the body, both in movement and in stationary positions.
   c. *Coordination:* The ability to integrate muscle motions into an efficient pattern of movement.
   d. *Power:* The ability to release maximum force or to contract the muscles in the shortest possible time.
   e. *Reaction Time:* The time it takes to perceive a stimulus and begin movement.

2. While going through and defining the above components, have the students name 3 to 5 sports requiring that skill to participate. (See the "3 to 5 Sports Worksheet.") Keep the list they come up with for the next activity. **Approximate time: Included in procedure step 1 above.**

3. In groups, assign students certain sports and activities and ask them to write down on the worksheet provided what performance-related components are required to participate at a beginner, intermediate, and advanced level of competition. Have them rank in importance the components for each activity. Let each group put their findings on the board and discuss the results. **Approximate time: 10 to 15 minutes.**

4. Have students use the worksheet provided to create a list, either as a class or in their groups, of exercises that will help to develop the specific components of performance-related fitness. **Approximate time: 10 minutes.**

5. Review with the students the health-related fitness components and discuss the similarities/differences between the two groups. **Approximate time: 20 minutes.**

6. Have the students use the worksheet provided to create a list of activities that

utilize part of both the health-related and performance-related components. **Approximate time: 10 minutes.**

Homework Assignments:

Depending upon the time allotted, some of the above activities may also be considered as homework assignments.

Name _____

3 TO 5 SPORTS WORKSHEET

For each of the following components, list 3 to 5 activities/sports requiring a moderate to high degree of that component to participate.

Agility:

Balance:

Coordination:

Power:

Reaction Time:

BEGINNER, INTERMEDIATE, AND ADVANCED LEVELS

Using the sports/activities you were assigned, write what performance-related components are required to participate at the beginner, intermediate, and advanced levels of competition. List the components in **order of importance** (most important listed first).

Sport/Activity: _____

Beginner-level components:

Intermediate-level components:

Advanced-level components:

Sport/Activity: _____

Beginner-level components:

Intermediate-level components:

Advanced-level components:

Sport/Activity: _____

Beginner-level components:

Intermediate-level components:

Advanced-level components:

Name _____

EXERCISES FOR PERFORMANCE-RELATED FITNESS

Create a list of exercises to help develop the following performance-related components:

Agility:

Balance:

Coordination:

Power:

Reaction Time:

ACTIVITIES USING HEALTH-RELATED AND PERFORMANCE-RELATED COMPONENTS

Create a list of activities that utilizes parts of both health-related and performance-related components.

PRINCIPLES OF EXERCISE (4-8)

Focus: Proper exercise principles

Equipment: Overhead projector, worksheets, pencils

Description:

Activities designed to demonstrate the principles of exercising and to help the students begin to integrate this knowledge into their daily activities.

Procedure:

1. Discuss with the students each of the principles of exercise listed and provide examples to help their understanding. **Approximate time: 30 to 50 minutes.**

    a. *Overload:* A person needs to do more than would normally be done to improve fitness. Muscles will not become stronger unless they are exercised at higher-than-normal levels. For example: If an individual is used to doing 25 Push-Ups a day, in order for him or her to develop greater upper-arm strength, that person must increase the number or type of Push-Up completed over a period of time.

    b. *Specificity:* A person needs to do specific exercises to improve specific components of physical fitness and specific body parts. In other words, specific exercises are needed for specific results. For example: Lifting weights will improve the specific muscles that are required for a particular lift, but it will not affect other muscles or other health-performance-related components, such as cardiovascular fitness.

    c. *Progression:* A person needs to start exercising slowly and continue to increase the amount of exercise done over a period of time. For example: In starting a jogging program, jog short distances and gradually increase the distance.

2. Have the students provide examples of how these principles apply to strength, muscular endurance, flexibility, and cardiovascular fitness.

Homework Assignments:

1. Have the students pick two specific exercises to perform for a week and have them keep a brief journal (see the "Exercise Journal" worksheet) of how they felt immediately afterwards and the next day. Sometimes the result of too much exercising is not felt for about 12 to 24 hours.

2. Assign the students two specific exercises to perform for a week and complete the same assignment as above. **You might want to pick unusual exercises that most students are not familiar with to allow them to experience the full importance of the exercise principles.**

EXERCISE JOURNAL (I)

ACTIVITY: _____

DURATION:

HOW I FELT IMMEDIATELY AFTER:

HOW I FELT THE NEXT MORNING:

HOW I FELT AFTER 24 HOURS:

ACTIVITY: _____

DURATION:

HOW I FELT IMMEDIATELY AFTER:

HOW I FELT THE NEXT MORNING:

HOW I FELT AFTER 24 HOURS:

Name _____

EXERCISE JOURNAL (II)

(This worksheet is to be used for the exercises assigned by the instructor.)

ACTIVITY: _____

DURATION:

HOW I FELT IMMEDIATELY AFTER:

HOW I FELT THE NEXT MORNING:

HOW I FELT AFTER 24 HOURS:

ACTIVITY: _____

DURATION:

HOW I FELT IMMEDIATELY AFTER:

HOW I FELT THE NEXT MORNING:

HOW I FELT AFTER 24 HOURS:

GUIDELINES FOR PHYSICAL FITNESS (4–8)

Focus: Guidelines for developing physical fitness

Equipment: Overhead projector, worksheets, pencils

Description:

Activities to enhance students' understanding of fitness concepts and how they can be applied to daily activities to improve students' individual fitness levels.

Procedure:

1. Discuss with the students each of the guidelines for physical fitness listed, and provide examples to help their understanding. **Approximate time: 30 minutes.**

   a. *Intensity:* How hard a person works out. This is related more to cardiovascular fitness, but also applies to other areas as well. For example: Are we working with minimal effort, 50% of our capabilities, or at 100%? This concept is sometimes hard for students to understand because it requires abstract cognition and perception of the percentages. One way to explain it would be: When the students finish their exercises, ask are they completely exhausted (indicating 85 to 100% effort)? tired, but can continue to work a little longer, or go to another task (indicating 60 to 85% effort)? or feel like they have done nothing (indicating minimal effort and little conditioning is taking place)?

   b. *Frequency:* How often one works out, that is, 3 days a week, 5 days, etc. Minimal recommendations are 3 to 4 days per week for moderate results.

   c. *Duration:* How long does the workout take? 30 minutes, 45 minutes, etc. Minimal recommendation is 20 to 30 minutes.

   d. *Mode of exercise:* What is the type of exercise being performed? High intensity, low intensity, heavy lifting, agility, etc. Some activities automatically require a higher level of training than others. Some are very specific to certain muscle groups and others are good for overall training. Students must decide on the mode of exercise, goals they want to achieve, and then figure the above three components.

2. Provide the students with a list of activities and have them place the activities into the following three categories without modifying any of the four guidelines. The categories are: activities that would normally be considered (1) low intensity, (2) moderate intensity, and (3) high intensity. For example: Walking is naturally a low intensity, while soccer is considered to be on the higher end of intensity. **Note:** Most activities will fall into the moderate category. Your students should also be telling you that depending upon the performer's expertise level and how hard he or she participates, most activities could fall into all three categories. (See the "Low, Moderate, High Worksheet.") **Approximate time: 20 minutes.**

3. Using the "Physical Fitness Questions" worksheet at the end of the activity, have the students adjust the workouts using the first three components. Provide some questions for the components that will allow you to check the students' understanding of the material presented. **Approximate time: 20 to 30 minutes. Could also be assigned as homework. Note:** The answers for the worksheet will vary.

Sample Questions:

- How could you modify someone's workout so he or she works at a higher rate (harder)? (*Answer:* increase the intensity)

- If I wanted a good workout, but my time was limited, how could I modify my workout to accomplish that goal? (*Answer:* Since time is short, increase the intensity or change the mode of activity by picking an activity requiring more effort.)

- I have been riding a stationary bicycle for 4 times/week, 30 minutes/workout, 50% exertion. Recently, I injured my ankle and had to quit working out for 3 weeks. I am now walking normally, but only for short distances before my ankle gets tired. Could you suggest a workout for me with my present condition? (*Answer:* The answers will vary as there are many possible solutions. Change the mode, try the bicycle for a shorter duration, etc.)

Name _____

LOW, MODERATE, HIGH WORKSHEET

Concept: Frequency, duration, intensity, and mode of exercise

Activities:

football	soccer	basketball
baseball	tennis	badminton
swimming	weight lifting	water skiing
snow skiing	sprint events	marathon running
high jumping	pole vaulting	volleyball
wrestling	ice hockey	walking
gymnastics	bicycling	diving

Instructions: Place each activity in the following categories where it is most likely to fit. "Low" indicates it takes minimal effort to participate at an **intermediate level;** "Moderate" indicates it takes approximately 50% effort; "High" indicates it takes a **high level of exertion** to perform.

LOW   *MODERATE*   *HIGH*

_____

_____

_____

_____

_____

_____

_____

_____

PHYSICAL FITNESS QUESTIONS

Concept: Frequency, duration, intensity, and mode of exercise

Instructions: Using the following workout, answer the questions.

I jog 4 times/week, 25 minutes, 60% intensity, 2 miles.

1. If I want to increase my endurance (the ability to go longer), what adjustments could I make?

   _____

   _____

2. If I want to increase my heart rate, what adjustments could I make?

   _____

   _____

3. If I want to complete the workout in a shorter time but not lose any benefits, what adjustments could I make?

   _____

   _____

4. I have just recovered from a serious respiratory illness. What adjustments could I make for continuing to work out?

   _____

   _____

   _____

CARDIOVASCULAR FITNESS (4-8)

Focus: Cardiovascular fitness

Equipment: Overhead projector, worksheets, pencils, stopwatches

Description:

Activities designed to provide the students with practical application to understanding the concept of cardiovascular fitness and how it applies to their lifestyle.

Procedure:

1. Provide a lecture on the anatomy of the heart and how the blood flows, concentrating on the flow to the muscles as well as talking about why the heart rate increases during certain activities. **Approximate time: 20 minutes.**

2. Make an overhead of "Cardiovascular Fitness Information" and discuss it with students. **Approximate time: 10 minutes.**

3. Briefly review the principles of exercise and guidelines for physical fitness, using the overhead or handouts. **Approximate time: 15 minutes.**

4. Ask the students to list some activities that would promote cardiovascular fitness. (See the "Cardiorespiratory Endurance Activities" overhead.) **Approximate time: 5 to 7 minutes.**

5. Teach the students how to take the heart rate at the neck (carotid) and at the wrist (brachial). Be certain to emphasize not using the thumb, as it has its own pulse. When taking the pulse at the neck, emphasize using only slight pressure. Have the students take their own heart rate. Have them record three trials at different times. (See "The Pulse" worksheet for instructions.) Then have them compare their rates with other students and discuss why there are differences. **Approximate time: 10 to 12 minutes.**

6. Discuss with the students the different heart rate measurements. Then teach them how to figure each measure using the "Heart Rate Measurements" worksheet.

   a. **Resting heart rate:** This should usually be determined first thing in the morning before getting out of bed. It is the period of time when individuals are most relaxed and refreshed. It should be taken for a full minute to get an accurate count. When at school, you can get a fairly accurate resting heart rate by having the students lie down quietly for approximately 5 minutes before taking.

   b. **Maximum heart rate:** This is the highest you would ever want your heart to beat during exercise. If this rate is reached, you are actually putting too much pressure on your heart and causing added stress. Individuals who are exercising at this rate should slow down. To find your maximum heart rate, use the formula: 220 – your age. Notice that as an individual gets older, his or her maximum heart rate decreases.

   c. **Target heart rate zone:** This is also referred to as the training zone for aerobic activities. It is the range you should strive to achieve when exercising. Based on the following formula, each student should be able to determine his or her own zone. The zone ranges are between 65% at the lower end and 80% at the upper end of maximum heart rate. Highly trained individuals can be expected to attain 90% at the upper end, while extremely sedentary individuals or those just beginning an aerobic program would start at the lower end. (See the "Heart Rate Measurements" worksheet to teach the formula to the students.)

7. Have the students run in place for two minutes. Then immediately take their heart rates. (See the "Aerobic Heart Rate" worksheet.) Record on the worksheet and answer the questions. **Approximate time: 10 minutes.**

8. Discuss with students other factors not related to physical activity that would make their heart beat faster. For example: stress, fear, etc. **Approximate time: 5 to 7 minutes.**

Cardiovascular Fitness Information

Why build cardiovascular endurance?

- Strengthen the heart and lungs

- Burn fat and control body composition

- Shape and firm muscles

- Lessen tension

- Help build self-esteem

What is a cardiovascular fitness activity?

- A continuous rhythm-type activity

- Activity done continuously for 15 to 60 minutes

- Entire body is moving

- Heart is beating faster than at rest

What should I remember?

- Progression: longer, faster, farther, often

- Regularity: 3–5 days/week all year

Cardiorespiratory Endurance Activities

- Aerobic Dance
- Cross-Country Skiing
- Cycling
- Interval Running
- Jogging

- Roller Skating
- Rope Skipping
- Swimming
- Walking

Some sports activities can help build cardiorespiratory endurance:

- Basketball
- Field Hockey (all positions except goalie)
- Handball
- Racquetball
- Soccer (all positions except goalie)
- Team Handball
- Tennis

THE PULSE

Sit quietly for 30 seconds. When instructed to begin, use the carotid (neck) method and take your pulse 3 times. (Wait 1 minute between each trial.) Record the number of beats you feel in:

a. 30 seconds: _____ × 2   = _____ beats/minute

b. 6 seconds: _____ add a "0" = _____ beats/minute

c. 60 seconds: _____   = _____ beats/minute

Were you within 5 beats/minute on all three results? _____

If not, what could cause the discrepancy?

_____

_____

_____

_____

Compare your "60-second" heart rate with another student's. Was there more than a 5-beat/minute difference in your rates? Why do you think there might be?

_____

_____

_____

_____

_____

_____

_____

Heart Rate Measurements

1. **Resting heart rate:** Lie on your back quietly for 4 to 6 minutes. Find your pulse and count each beat for 1 minute. Do it two different times to get a more accurate score. If you are more than 5 beats apart from the first time and the second time, take a third time and average.

   1st recording: _____   2nd recording: _____   3rd recording: _____

2. **Maximum heart rate:** This is the highest rate your heart should be working. If you are at or above this mark when exercising, you are putting **too much** pressure/stress on your heart. Slow down!

   220 – your age = maximum heart rate

   What's yours? _____

3. **Target heart rate zone:** This is also known as the training zone for aerobic activities. The zone you should be exercising in is between 65% and 80% of your maximum heart rate. Use the formula below to figure your own personal zone.

   Personal maximum heart rate – resting heart rate = _____ (A)

   (A) times .65 = _____+ your resting rate = (lower limit)

   (A) times .80 = _____+ your resting rate = (upper limit)

   What is your target heart rate? _____

AEROBIC HEART RATE

Beats/minute after jogging for 2 minutes (6-second method): _____

Beats/minute after resting for 2 minutes (6-second method): _____

Is this last resting rate within 5 beats/minute of your Target Heart Rate Zone?_____

What reasons could you give for it not being within the 5-beat range?

_____

_____

_____

_____

_____

_____

_____

_____

_____

_____

_____

_____

_____

_____

AEROBIC AND ANAEROBIC FITNESS (4-8)

Focus: Aerobic/anaerobic fitness

Equipment: Overhead projector

Description:

Activities designed to provide the students with practical application and understanding of the concept of aerobic and anaerobic fitness and how it applies to their lifestyles.

Activities:

1. Conduct a discussion of the differences between aerobic and anaerobic fitness. Discussion points should include how it can be enhanced, and physical and genetic factors. Review the activity "Guidelines for Physical Fitness." **Approximate time: 20 to 30 minutes.**

   a. *Aerobic:* Meaning *with* oxygen, these activities are of low to moderate intensity for extended periods of time. Cardiovascular fitness can be enhanced through progressive activity, but is also somewhat limited by such genetic factors as type of muscles a person predominately inherits. Aerobic activities use slow twitch muscle fibers, and the activities should use the large muscle groups predominately.

   b. *Anaerobic:* Meaning *without* oxygen, these activities are of moderate to high intensity for short periods of time (maximum 3 to 4 minutes). Quick bursts of speed and power constitute anaerobic activities. Anaerobic capacity can be enhanced lightly with training, but there is still only a certain amount of activity that can be sustained before the body "hits the wall."

2. Based on the above discussion, have the students come up with a list of 5 to 7 activities that would fall into either aerobic or anaerobic categories.

Homework Assignment or Class Project:

Have the students do research on their own on the differences between aerobic and anaerobic activities. Have them pick four activities they particularly enjoy participating in and discuss whether they are aerobic or anaerobic in nature. Have students also select several individual exercises and discuss why each exercise would be considered aerobic or anaerobic in nature.

MUSCULAR STRENGTH AND ENDURANCE (4-8)

Focus: Muscular strength and endurance

Equipment: Overhead projector, worksheets, pencils

Description:

Activities designed to provide students with practical and theoretical applications to understanding the concepts of muscular strength and endurance. Students differentiate types of strength conditioning and learn how to enhance particular activities/sports participation.

Procedure:

1. Have a brief discussion on how the muscles work in relation to anatomy and joints. Include in the discussion the following questions: Are all muscles alike? Which muscles need to be the strongest and why? Which muscles do we seldom use and why? **Approximate time: 15 minutes.**

2. Discuss the following terms and their relationship to the guidelines for physical fitness and principles of exercise. (See the overhead transparency.) **Approximate time: 15 to 30 minutes.**

   a. *Muscular Strength:* The amount of force a muscle or muscle group can exert in one maximal effort. For example: One time of lifting a barbell at the maximum load. To increase, use heavier weights with less repetitions.

   b. *Muscular Endurance:* The amount of force a muscle or muscle group can exert over a period of time. For example: Repeated lifting at a specified weight. To increase, use lighter weight with more repetitions.

Note:

In order to increase both strength and endurance, you have to change the weight, time, and repetitions. At the end of a set, you should feel as if some work has been done, but not to the point of exhaustion. It is recommended that if an individual can perform 3 sets of 10 and feel only minimally worked, he or she should increase the weight by 5 pounds.

   c. *Isotonic or Dynamic Contraction:* A visible shortening or lengthening of a muscle. You can see the movement.

   d. *Isometric or Static Contraction:* A shortening or lengthening of a muscle without necessarily being visible. The muscle is working but you can't actually see the movement. For example: Pushing against an immovable object. The muscles are working, but you cannot see the movement.

   e. *Isokinetic Contraction:* A muscle contraction with equal resistance through a full range of motion. For example: Performing a biceps curl with a weight in your hand.

Note:

Stress that girls will not build bulk from weight training because they lack the necessary male hormone, testerone, in sufficient quantity, that is necessary to build bulk.

3. Have students compare and contrast isotonic, isometric, and isokinetic training. Give advantages and disadvantages of each on the worksheet provided. **Approximate time: 10 minutes.**

4. Give students a list of activities (see the "Activities and Muscle Groups" worksheet) and have them write the muscle group(s) each activity primarily uses. **Approximate time: 15 minutes.**

5. Assign the students three or four of the activities from the "Activities and Muscle Groups" worksheet and have them list on the worksheet provided four exercises they would recommend using to develop muscular strength for that activity. **Approximate time: 15 minutes.**

6. Give each student a small piece of clay. Have the student knead it, then discuss whether it was easier to mold at first or after being worked for awhile. Compare this to exercising our muscles. **Approximate time: 5 to 10 minutes.**

Muscular Strength

Why build muscular strength?

- Perform physical activities, such as lifting and moving

- Replace fat with muscle

- Shape and firm your body

- Help build self-esteem

What is an exercise to build muscular strength?

- A controlled exercise using resistance in particular muscles

- Performing a limited number of repetitions with maximum resistance

- Moving only a limited number of joints

- The muscle group being exercised is working harder

What should I remember?

- **Progression:** Adding resistance, doing more repetitions or sets, working out more often

- **Regularity:** 3 to 5 days per week all year long

- **Overload:** Use near-maximum resistance and few repetitions (strength); use lower resistance and higher repetitions (endurance)

ISOMETRIC, ISOTONIC, AND ISOKINETIC

Give an advantage and disadvantage of each of the following types of strength training.

Isometric

_____

_____

_____

Isotonic

_____

_____

_____

Isokinetic

_____

_____

_____

© 1994 by Parker Publishing Company

QUESTIONS: Use the back of this sheet for your answers.
1. Linda has just finished working out and is completely exhausted. She feels as if she cannot even make it to the car to get home. What would you recommend she do for the next 3 to 5 days?
2. John has just come to you bragging that he has just completed 6 sets of 10 bench presses, lifting 75 pounds, as well as 6 sets of 10 bicep curls, lifting 30 pounds. He states that he feels great and could probably complete another 5 or 6 sets of each. Is John increasing his muscular strength and endurance? Why or why not? What recommendation would you make to John to get better results from his workout?

ACTIVITIES AND MUSCLE GROUPS

Beside each of the following activities, list which of these four muscle groups are predominately used. Use the letters.

A. Upper body   B. Lower body   C. Abdominal   D. Combination of them

____ football

____ soccer

____ gymnastics

____ pole vaulting

____ baseball

____ weightlifting

____ bicycling

____ wrestling

____ swimming

____ jogging

____ volleyball

____ snow skiing

Name _____

APPROPRIATE EXERCISES TO DEVELOP MUSCULAR STRENGTH

After you have been assigned four activities, list three exercises you would recommend to enhance participation in that particular activity. For example: diving—mountain climbing, flexibility, curl-ups, and arm circles.

Activity   **Exercises**

_____

_____

_____

_____

_____

_____

_____

_____

_____

_____

_____

_____

BODY COMPOSITION (4-8)

Focus: Body composition, its relation to health, how to measure it

Equipment: Overhead projector, worksheets, pencils

Description:

Activities designed to give students practical and theoretical application to aid in understanding the relationship of body composition and a healthy lifestyle. Nutrition concepts and exercises are also provided to demonstrate the relationship between nutrition and body composition.

Procedure:

1. Have a general discussion on the meaning of body composition, discussing the terms listed and the information provided. **Approximate time: 15 to 20 minutes.**

   a. *Body composition:* The relative percentages of fat and fat-free body mass.

   b. The average male = 10 to 15% body fat; the average female = 15 to 20% body fat.

   c. *Obese:* An individual who has an excessive amount of body fat; 20% over ideal weight.

   d. Lean tissue is heavier than fat tissue; therefore, a person can be over their ideal weight and still not be fat.

2. Discuss the negative effects of obesity on the skeletal system, cardiovascular system, and appearance. **Approximate time: 15 minutes.**

3. Have students research three different methods of measuring body composition. Write a report on the advantages and disadvantages of each method.

4. Have students analyze caloric intake for several days to discover their nutritional habits. Use the worksheet provided for guidelines. Students can find caloric analysis of food in most health books.

5. Have students evaluate nutritional data related to fast foods, fad diets as they relate to weight control, fitness, and proper nutrition. The information can be found in most of the fast-food restaurants or in calorie-counting books.

Name _____

CALORIC INTAKE OF FOOD

DAY: 1   2   3   (circle one)

TIME	FOOD EATEN	QUANTITY	CALORIES

FLEXIBILITY (4–8)

Focus: Flexibility and its importance in everyday activities

Equipment: Overhead projector, worksheets, pencils

Description:

Activities designed to give students practical and theoretical applications in understanding the concept of flexibility.

Procedure:

1. Review anatomical and muscle structure. Discuss with the students the definition of flexibility, and why it is important to maintain. ***Flexibility:*** The ability of a joint to move through a full range of motion.

   - ***Reasons to maintain flexibility:*** prevents injury, increases mobility, better circulation. Use the "Daily Flexibility Program" transparency to aid in the discussion.
   - Discuss the difference between exercise that increases flexibility and exercise that is used for a warm-up.
   - Flexibility should be done on a daily basis, 5 to 10 minutes, 2 times a day, especially as a person gets older and his or her activities slow down.
   - When performing flexibility exercises, maintain the *static* position for 15 to 30 seconds. No bouncing! **Approximate time: 20 to 30 minutes.**

2. Have students make a poster or list of activities that require a high degree of flexibility. For example: gymnastics, pole vaulting, etc. This can be a homework assignment or you can have the materials on hand to do in class. **Approximate time: posterboard, 60 minutes; lists, 15 to 30 minutes.**

3. Have students list specific exercises to develop flexibility for certain body regions. See the "flexibility" worksheet for instructions. **Approximate time: 15 minutes.**

4. Have the students perform the "Self-Test" for flexibility, and determine their own capabilities. Once completed, have them design a program to maintain or improve their flexibility. Have them compare their results with several other members of the class and try to come to some generalizations about gender and flexibility, and joint differences with regard to flexibility. **Approximate time: 30 to 45 minutes.**

Note:

There are some standardized flexibility tests available. Try to purchase or borrow these if possible; if not, the self-test is a good substitute.

Some questions to stimulate the discussion might include:

- Was there any noticeable flexibility difference between females and males with regard to the self-test?
- How does anatomical structure play a role in flexibility?
- What are some factors that might determine the flexibility of an individual?

5. Assign students to lead/demonstrate various stretches for specific joints or muscle groups that will increase flexibility. (See the "Top Ten Stretching Activities" worksheet.) **Approximate time: daily, 5 minutes.**

6. Discuss with the students the importance of proper body alignment (posture) and its benefits for physical activity as well as daily activities.

Homework Assignments:

1. Have students talk to professionals who work in the athletic training, physical therapy, or sports medicine fields about types and frequency of injuries related to limited flexibility.

2. Have students research various flexibility programs/techniques. Have them prepare a paper addressing the issues of similarities, differences, advantages, disadvantages, and practicality with regard to equipment required.

Daily Flexibility Program

Why it increases flexibility

- Prepares the body's joints, muscles, and connective tissue for more vigorous activity

- Helps reduce the risk of injury during activity

- Increases the range of motion of each joint

- Increased flexibility will improve your ability to perform

Points of emphasis

- Slow stretching is best; don't bounce or jerk

- Stretch each joint of the body in all directions the joint moves

- Breathe while stretching; inhale while recovering; exhale slowly during stretch

- Increase the range of motion in each joint over a period of weeks

- Stretch daily

Remember, warm-up exercises are not the same as exercises to increase flexibility!

FLEXIBILITY

Under each body region, list at least three exercises you would recommend to help maintain or increase flexibility.

Upper body region: shoulders and neck

_____

_____

_____

_____

Trunk region: back and abdomen

_____

_____

_____

_____

Lower body region: hips, knees, and ankles

_____

_____

_____

_____

SELF-TEST

Write a definition of flexibility from your dictionary. Use the back of this sheet for your answer. What degree of flexibility do you have?

	I can do it easily	I can do it barely	I cannot do it at all
Sit down with your legs straight, heels 6 inches apart. Slowly reach forward and touch your ankles.			
Same as above, but touch your toes.			
Place your left forearm behind your back, bent, palm facing out with fingers pointing up. Place your right arm over and behind your right shoulder; touch your left hand. Repeat, changing arm positions.			
Lying on your back, slowly bend your right leg over your left while keeping your shoulders and hands on the ground. Repeat, moving the other leg.			
Stand with arms extended overhead and palms facing out, back of the hands touching. Stretch your arms upward and slightly back; hold for 8 to 10 seconds.			

Top Ten Stretching Activities

REMEMBER: **Stretch slowly, breathe slowly, and cover a full range of motion**

- Shoulder Circles

- Side Stretch

- Back Stretch

- Neck Stretch

- Knee Raises

- Quadriceps Stretch

- Achilles Stretch

- Ankle Stretch

- Hip Stretch (Forward)

- Hip Stretch (Lateral)

DIET AND EXERCISE (4–8)

Focus: Proper diet and exercise

Equipment: worksheets, pencils

Description:

Activities designed to provide the students with practical application to understanding some of the concepts related to proper diet and exercise and how they apply to their lifestyle.

Procedure:

1. Have the students split into groups of four to six. Provide them with magazines and have them make a poster of the foods they usually eat. **Approximate time: one or two class periods. You may also assign this as a homework assignment.** *Note:* Do not preface this assignment with a lecture on proper nutrition.

2. Have the students place the posters on the wall when completed. Then have each group analyze a different group's poster. When analyzing the poster, the group should be making two lists: a list of healthy foods and a list of unhealthy foods. **Approximate time: 15 to 20 minutes.**

3. Compile a master list on the board or overhead from all the groups and see what commonalities appear. **Approximate time: 15 to 25 minutes.**

4. Conclude with a discussion on the benefits of healthy foods and the disadvantages of unhealthy foods. (This ties in with some of the other concept activities, especially "Body Composition.") **Approximate time: 20 to 30 minutes.**

Homework Assignments:

1. Have the students analyze their eating patterns during the weekdays by completing the "Caloric Intake Record" worksheet at the end of the activity. They should note all categories. You could do this activity for one to three days.

2. Have the students repeat the previous activity, this time charting their eating habits on a weekend. Then have them compare the two cycles of patterns and write a brief report of their conclusions. Include in the report possible changes that could be used in a goal-setting process.

3. Have the students keep track of all the activities they participate in for 3 to 5 days. Have them complete the "Energy Expenditure Record." Once completed, have them write a report on "Do I exercise enough?" based on the findings from their chart.

4. Have students prepare an "Energy Expenditure Record" on a weekend and compare the difference in their activity levels.

CALORIC INTAKE RECORD

INSTRUCTIONS: Keep track of the food you eat for a period of three to five days, completing the chart below. You will need to make an approximation of the quantity and then look up the number of calories in a "calorie counter book." These books can usually be found in the library or at any book store.

Name: _____   DAY: **M   T   W   TH   F   SA   SU**

(Circle one)

TIME	FOOD ITEM	QUANTITY EATEN	CALORIES
9:30 a.m.	APPLE	1 MEDIUM	100

Name: _____   DAY: **M   T   W   TH   F   SA   SU**

(Circle one)

TIME	FOOD ITEM	QUANTITY EATEN	CALORIES
9:30 a.m.	APPLE	1 MEDIUM	100

ENERGY EXPENDITURE RECORD

Instructions: Keep track of your daily activities for a period of three days and fill in the chart. When noting the **value,** use the scale below. A sample has been given to help you get started.

1 = low level of energy required to complete task
2 = moderate level of energy required to complete task
3 = high level of energy required to complete task

TIME	ACTIVITY	DURATION	VALUE
8:00 a.m.	got dressed	20 minutes	1.5
8:30 a.m.	ate breakfast	10 minutes	1

Name _____   Day: **M   T   W   TH   F   SA   SU**

(circle one)

ENERGY EXPENDITURE RECORD

TIME	ACTIVITY	DURATION	VALUE

5

Communications and Special Programs

Positive Communications and Activities

Throughout the years educators have looked to the public for support of their programs. In an effort to gain this support we have developed numerous techniques and programs designed to highlight the successful application of instruction through the use of student demonstrations, parent newsletters, and the visual media. Section 5 presents numerous activities that have proven to be successful in "spreading the word" about our quality programs and that will spark your imagination. In addition to the formal lines of communication, we must look at "special" programs designed for students. Of these special programs, the use of student-centered field days or play days is most common. Presented are basic organizations and activity concepts designed to spark the reader's imagination.

COMMUNICATIONS

To communicate the positive aspects, goals, and successes of the program, all teachers should be utilizing positive and effective communication techniques so the program is understood and supported.

The most effective communication instrument for physical education is the *quality* of the program itself. The reports students carry home about knowledge and skills learned will create a high regard for the quality program.

Other means of disseminating information about the program are:

- Student demonstrations
- Informational brochures and newsletters
- Informational presentations
- Parent involvement
- Periodic reports of student progress
- Relevant homework

STUDENT DEMONSTRATIONS

Activity demonstrations are extensively used by physical educators to provide an effective method to communicate the physical education program to parents and the general community. Through these performances, it is easy to promote the success of your student-centered program.

Demonstrations can be conducted on special occasions, such as Open-House Night, PTSA Meetings, Spring Programs, etc. No matter what the occasion, they should be planned as an integral part of the total physical education program.

Demonstrations should represent the regular physical education program. They should involve all, or as many as possible, students rather than a few exceptional performers. Preparation for the demonstration should not interfere with the regular instructional program, but should be an outgrowth of that program. The purpose of these programs is to inform the public—through a demonstration of student knowledge and skill—in addition to entertain. The following is a sample outline of what a demonstration program might contain.

Sample Parent-Night Demonstration (Grades K–6)

7:00 p.m. Videotape of regular classes is shown while parents are entering the performance area.

Brochures outlining the performance schedule and the physical education program are handed out by students.

7:15 Introduction of the program—what is quality physical education and how our program meets these outcomes.

What parents will be seeing (regular activities taught in the physical education classes for each grade).

7:30 Opening—large group. Representative from each grade level performs various individual skills on small apparatus; e.g., juggling, jump rope, pogo stick, footbags, unicycles, roller skates, etc.

After two minutes of "freestyle" performance, a group is at each station to show a learning progression for the equipment; e.g., rope skipping—basic two-foot jump, front straddle, side straddle, skier, bell, etc.

7:45 Grades K–2—Dance

- "Fiddle Around"
- "Bird Dance"
- "Shindig in the Barn"

8:00 Grades 3–4—Fitness

- Stretching Warm-up
- "Aerobic Circuit"
- Walking Cool-Down

8:15 Grade 5—Tumbling and Rope Skipping

- Basic Tumbling: forward rolls (squat, standing, straddle, jump), backward rolls (squat, standing, straddle, jump), include different dismounts. Have a line of mats, end to end, with students on both sides. When the signal to "go" is given, students on both sides begin their rolls towards the other side, finishing with a dismount and 180-degree turn.

- Basic Strength Moves: 3-point tip-up, supported handstand, etc.
- Walk overs, bridges, etc.
- Rope Skipping: 3-minute freestyle routines. Have students perform in groups of 3. The announcer calls out students' names and the movements they are doing.

8:30   Grade 6—Tumbling and Rope Skipping

- Using the line of mats have students perform cartwheels, handsprings, etc., the length of the mat. Conclude with the group walking on their hands for a specified length.
- Rope Skipping—Double Dutch. Basic routines, moving towards partner routines, speed jumping, and gymnastic moves into and out of the ropes; e.g., cartwheel in/out, round off into cartwheel, out.

8:45   Conclusion—All students come out and jog one lap around the facility, stopping in the front. Thank the audience and students. Compliment students on a quality program and thank the parents for their support of a quality program.

          Indicate that you will be available for questions.

8:50   Play the physical education class video as parents leave.

Some organizations are very adamant on limiting the length of a program. If you are limited by time, here is a sample program.

4th Grade

7:00   Same as above

7:15   Same as above

7:20   Fitness Activity (aerobic routine)

7:25   Large Group Activity (parachute)

7:35   Dance ("Virginia Reel")

7:50   Conclusion—Large Group Activity (jump rope)

7:55   Concluding Statements

After each performance, place a follow-up note on the success of the program in the school newsletter. This "article" should contain information on the type of performance, the activities involved, and the numbers and classes of students performing. Thank all those who participated and invite anyone who was unable to attend to visit a class and see the students "in action."

Regardless of the amount of time, it is important to have some type of demonstration night at least once a year—more if possible. Scheduling a demonstration three times a year with different grades works quite well. Parents and relatives enjoy watching their children and it is a perfect way to educate them about the importance of physical activity. These programs should be fun and informational. All participants, the audience, and staff should feel excited and ready to continue promoting a quality program.

INFORMATIONAL BROCHURES AND NEWSLETTERS

The most efficient method of contacting a large percentage of the community is through informational brochures and newsletters. Both of these methods can be utilized to promote a specific event or activity, or as a general periodic form of communication.

An informational brochure is traditionally used to promote the general program. The content focuses on program philosophy and goals, student expectations, activities to be taught, special events/programs, and program highlights. Recently, program brochures have included a section on quality programming, highlighting what a quality physical education program is and offering a check list for parents to compare the school program to professional standards. By using this method it has been found that parents take the time to examine the program, thus becoming more familiar with it, and becoming more involved and supportive.

The distribution of the informational brochure should be done during the initial week of school via the students or a general mailing. In addition, brochures should be available in the school office and at PTSA meetings, etc. Distribution to the community can be made in accordance with school district policy and procedure.

Sample Informational Brochure

Elementary
Physical Education

A Basic

Aspect Of Education

In The

Olympic Public Schools

Jeff Carpenter & Diane Tunnell
Physical Education Specialists

(front cover)

PHILOSOPHY OF PROGRAM:

In the past, many people have considered the physical education program within the school system to be a "necessary evil." There is little doubt that a number of students and parents have come in contact with a "throw out the ball" approach to this important portion of the curriculum. To many, this experience has influenced the way they feel about <u>any</u> physical education program.

The primary concern of the Olympic physical education staff is the individual. Accordingly, the program is structured to meet the needs of each student on an individual basis in order for everyone to experience success at their own level. Thus, the primary emphasis which permeates the physical education programs in Olympic consists of physical fitness and skill development to enhance the quality of health for vocational and leisure pursuits.

BASIS OF ELEMENTARY PROGRAMS:

Physical education at the elementary level is taught primarily by the classroom teacher. Program planning is the responsibility of the physical education specialist who also assists the classroom teacher with a minimum of one demonstration lesson per week. The demonstration lesson is designed to help implement the program through the demonstration of specific skills and teaching techniques. The classroom teacher follows up the demonstration lesson with daily lessons emphasizing the skills and activities presented. Specific skills, games and activities have been allocated to each grade level to assure a sequential program. A copy of these guidelines has been given to each teacher as a resource in carrying out their weekly program.

(inside pages)

PROGRAM EMPHASIS AND OFFERINGS:

PRIMARY GRADES:

The major objectives at the primary level (Grades K–2) are to develop basic manipulative skills and to develop basic strength, endurance and coordination of the large body muscles. These elements are developed during the daily 20–30 minute session of physical education.

September: Ball Skills—Movement Concepts—Fitness
October: Soccer—Basic Tumbling
November: Scooters—Manipulative Skills (Using balls, bean bags, and
            individual apparatus)
December: Rhythms—Parachute—Individual Apparatus (Tug ropes,
            hoops, wands and skip ropes)
January: Gymnastics—Tumbling—Stunts—Apparatus
February: Rhythm—Tumbling—Stunts
March: Manipulative Skills
April: T-Ball—Fitness—Track & Field
May: Track & Field—Fitness

INTERMEDIATE GRADES:

The program objectives at the intermediate level (grades 3–5) continue the emphasis on strength, endurance and coordination while gradually shifting from basic skills to a specific sport skill emphasis.

September: Fitness—Football
October: Soccer
November: Basketball—Volleyball
December: Volleyball—Tumbling
January: Gymnastics—Rhythms—Tumbling
February: Apparatus—Combatives
March: Team Handball—Hockey
April: Softball—Track
May: Track & Field—Fitness

(inside pages)

CHARACTERISTICS OF A QUALITY PROGRAM:

1) All students actively participating

2) Students displaying respect and consideration for others

3) Students showing enthusiasm about activities

4) Students using equipment and supplies appropriately

5) Students working on task

6) Students pursuing physical education activities during free time

The elementary physical education staff of the Olympic School District feels the Olympic program meets these qualities and invites all members of the community to visit the programs at any time.

A slide presentation depicting the total elementary physical education program is available for viewing by any school or community group. If you or your group wish to view this interesting 20-minute program please contact the physical education staff by calling 555–1100.

(back cover)

PHYSICAL EDUCATION NEWSLETTER

Whether your newsletter is a district or individual school publication, it is used to highlight ongoing accomplishments and upcoming activities and events. Each newsletter should contain sections on program highlights, spotlight activities, quality effort and performance by students, a family activity, and a message from the teacher.

Sample Ideas for Newsletter Sections

- *Program Highlights:* Provide an outline of grade-level activities that were presented during the time period since the last publication. Keep it short but offer enough detail to provide information that parents want to know.
- *Spotlight Activities:* What did the students like the best? Put in quotes from students at each grade level; e.g., Grade 5, Jonathan C. "This week we rode unicycles around a series of cones. After doing a figure-8 individually, we held hands with a partner and did the figure-8."
- *Quality Efforts:*
  Grade 6, Brad T.: Improved 10% in his juggling score.
  Grade 3, Taylor P.: Did 10 modified pull-ups.
  Grade 4, Brenda T.: Scored 3 goals in a floor hockey game.
- *Family Activity:* Read an article in the newspaper or in a magazine related to health/fitness. Discuss the article while taking a 20-minute walk. While watching TV, do an exercise every time a commercial comes on, such as stretching, curl-ups, push-ups, etc.
- *Future Activities:* Provide a calendar of events for the time period between this communication and the next.
- *Teacher Message:* Write a short message thanking people who have volunteered or supported the program, ask for assistance in some event, invite parents to participate in classes with their children, or write about a problem and possible solutions.

Regardless of how a newsletter is formatted, parents will respond in a positive manner when presented ongoing, student-centered information.

INFORMATIONAL PRESENTATIONS

Presentations made to various community groups provide an excellent opportunity to develop a broad base of support for physical education programs. In planning these presentations the informational needs of the audience must be taken into consideration. Some groups may be interested in hearing about how fitness is developed and tested, others may want to know about student expectations and program outcomes, while still others may desire knowledge regarding program needs. No matter what their interest, the presentation must be specifically designed and focused on their interests.

During the presentation it is important, as it is with teaching a class, to utilize a variety of techniques. These techniques may include the use of visuals (*quality* overheads, and/or slides—videos should only be used if a large projection screen is available so that the entire audience will be able to clearly see), a simple activity (have the audience touch their toes and hold the position for 10 seconds, slowly stand, spread feet shoulder-width apart, bend knees to a 45-degree angle and hold for 30 seconds, slowly stand, bend forward, and touch the floor; if all goes well they should be able to "stretch further than before," ask why), small student demonstrations, posters of actual students performing, and an informational brochure to be given to all participants. It is possible to have students perform for a short period of time at the informational presentations. This allows the group to see actual activities and skills tied to the verbal presentation.

At the conclusion of the presentation, ask participants to visit the physical education classes and to ask questions. While they may appear stressful, these programs can be a great deal of fun and will expand the base of support for physical education.

Sample Groups

- Service Organizations
- Community Clubs
- Medical Associations or Local Medical Groups
- City Councils
- Neighborhood Groups
- School Boards
- State Professional Education Organizations (principals, school directors, school boards, etc.)
- State PTSA Organization

Sample Presentation Format

- What is a quality physical education program.
- What is the district/school philosophy of physical education.
- What are the developmental needs of students at the age you are dealing with.
- What is the professional staff qualifications.
- What should a community member (the audience) look for in a quality program.
- Speak to common "myths" regarding physical education:

    children get enough exercise during recess and after school

    most children are physically fit

    children learn enough activity skills outside of school

    physical education does not teach knowledge leading towards healthy lifestyles

    physical education is a separate part of a child's "basic education"

- How your program is providing quality learning experiences for all children.

PARENT INVOLVEMENT

The implementation of quality educational programs requires a cooperative effort involving educators and parents. Although parents may, at times, seem distant and/or negative, each one has a desire to assist in providing a quality education for their children. To provide opportunities for them to become actively involved, teachers must first ask parent involvement and provide opportunities that are flexible enough to meet work schedules and fit into their abilities and interest levels. As a rule of thumb, parents prefer to be active with students rather than assisting through data-entry tasks.

Sample Parental Involvement Activities

- Assisting in physical education classes.
- Assisting with physical fitness testing (manage stations).
- Assisting with school field-day events.
- Assisting with student demonstrations and informational presentations.
- Doing work at home: data entry, record sheets, certificate design.

No matter what activity parents participate in, it is important to maintain a positive attitude and remember that they are giving of their time to assist you with their children.

PERIODIC REPORTS OF STUDENT PROGRESS

In addition to comments and grades related to student progress provided on regular school report cards, an excellent communication technique is to provide additional reports of student progress.

These reports take several different formats depending on the information being provided. Examples are:

- Individual Student Performance Task Cards
- Individual Fitness Report Forms
- "Good Job" notes on progress
- Certificates of Achievement
- Activity Journals

Sample Periodic Reports of Student Progress

1. **Individual Task Cards:** As a student completes a task card, sign it, make a positive comment, and send it home.
2. **Individual Fitness Report Forms:** There are numerous commercial fitness-reporting forms (the Prudential *Fitnessgram* from the Aerobic Institute for Aerobic Research and *Physical Best* from the American Alliance for

HPERD are two examples) that can be used to provide feedback to parents on fitness achievement. In addition to the commercial forms, you can develop your own using 4-copy carbonless paper. Here's an example.

		attempt #1	#2	#3
Item	**Score**			
Modified Pull-Up				
Curl-Up				
Mile Run/Walk				
V-Sit and Reach				
Body Composition				

NAME _____   AGE: _____

white (file), yellow (1st home), pink (2nd home), gold (3rd home)

3. **"Good Job" Notes:** A "good job" note is simply a quick handwritten note stating a success the student has had that day or week. Parents look forward to receiving these and students are extremely proud.

April 22

Just a short note to let you know that Kimberly improved in volleyball this week. At the beginning of the week she was unable to complete a serve over the net. Today she was successful 5 times. Super job Kimberly—KEEP UP THE GREAT WORK!

signed: _____

4. **Certificates of Achievement:** These certificates can be given out for any success a student has. They are best received if made at the school and signed by the physical education teacher, classroom teacher, and principal. Two samples are given on pages 338 and 339.

IMPROVEMENT AWARD

presented to:

__skill development
__cooperation
__physical fitness
__being cheerful
—effort

_____

*For outstanding improvement
in your physical education class*

_____
Teacher

_____
Date

5. ***Student Journals:*** This activity is extremely beneficial to students and parents alike. At the conclusion of each lesson provide time for the students to write a few notes on what activities they took part in, how they felt, and their achievements. For the elementary teacher, this activity could be done during the class time immediately following physical education, thus providing a "winding down" time to prepare students to resume classroom activities.

At the conclusion of each month or quarter, have students take their journals home, share them with parents and friends, and return them to school. At the end of the year, students can take time to review all the activities they have participated in during the year and write a summary of their accomplishments.

RELEVANT HOMEWORK

Enhancement of knowledge, skills, and fitness are not developed during the school day alone. Appropriate activities should be assigned to students on a regular basis, as homework, to keep them active and thinking about their lifestyle choices. Specific assignments can be made either on an individual basis or to the entire class. As noted in the following examples, activities have been designed to involve the students, friends, and family members. By expanding the number of participants, the positive activities taught in physical education are brought into the home and community to provide for a greater understanding and support of quality programs.

HIP TO BE FIT

WASHINGTON

Presented to:

in recognition of your high level achievement
in pursuit of physical fitness
and a healthy lifestyle.

Physical Education Teacher

Principal

SAMPLE HOMEWORK ASSIGNMENT

WEEK	MONDAY	TUESDAY	WEDNESDAY	THURSDAY	FRIDAY	SATURDAY
6	Find a picture of a bicept muscle. Think about how it works to help lift an object. Do 25 curl-ups and 3 sets with your hand weights.	Do 3 flexibility exercises for both legs and upper body.	Tape a long balloon to pieces of wood or heavy cardboard and make a model of an arm muscle. Do 25 curls × 3 sets with your hand weights.	Take a 10-minute jog and a 15-minute walk with a friend.	Do 20 curl-ups - or - modified curl-ups.	Eat a good breakfast, relax, and organize a family walk.
7	Find a picture of a person in a swim suit, identify the muscles, and discuss with your family how they work. Ride your bike for 30 minutes.	Jump rope for 3 minutes × 3 sets. Can you do 6 different steps?	Read an article on diet and exercise. Discuss with a friend your exercise program in relation to the article.	Ride your bike for 30 continuous minutes.	Check your diet for the day. Are you eating from the 4 food groups and in appropriate proportions? Take a 30-minute walk.	Sleep in and relax. Do 30 slow crab-kicks while watching TV.
8	Take a 15-minute jog and a 20-minute walk with family and friends.	Use your hand weights for your legs. Do 15 leg extensions × 5 sets.	Read the food ads in the paper. Plan a nutritious meal by cutting out ads. Do curl-ups - or - modified curl-ups.	Check with your family members about their exercise routines. Do at least one activity together.	Jump rope for 3 minutes × 3 sets. Do 7 different steps during each set.	Good job! Relax today and think about your future health.
9	Make an exercise plan for the next school year. What can you do after school each day? Ride your bike for 30 minutes.	Do 1 activity from your exercise plan. Write down how it went.	Check your diet. Can you keep it up each school lunch? What can you do to make sure? Do 20 push-ups or modified push-ups.	Do 2 different exercises from your personal exercise plan. Do you need to change anything?	Jump rope for 3½ minutes × 3 sets. Try not to miss. How many different steps did you use?	Relax and think positive thoughts about school. Take a 25-minute walk with friends.
10	Walk to your school and around the grounds—jog home. Can you do this each day during good weather?	Use your hand weights for both legs and arm curls—20 curls × 3 sets; press—20 overhead × 3 sets; leg curls—15 leg extensions × 5 sets.	Check your diet—make a nutritious sack lunch. Jog for 10 minutes with a friend.	Read a nutrition/fitness article. Take it to school next week and discuss it. Do 25 curl-ups or modified curl-ups.	Ride your bike for 30 continuous minutes.	Look over your exercise plan. Think positive thoughts about the school year and your health. IT'S UP TO YOU!

Sample Homework Assignments (Grades 6–8)

See the sample 5-week homework assignment sheet.

STUDENT-CENTERED FIELD PLAY DAYS

Planning and Organization:

Field Play Days are one of the highlights of the physical education program. These activities are usually conducted in the spring of each year and involve the entire school in success-oriented activities. There are numerous formats that can be used to conduct these programs; however, all of them have the following in common:

- Activities have been presented in the physical education classes or require low-level skills so that practice/experience will not affect the results.
- Active participation is highlighted and competition is downplayed.
- The implementation of the event requires cooperation from the entire staff along with parent or community volunteers.
- Recognition is given to all students who participate regardless of individual event ranking.

In order to conduct a well-organized and successful event, planning should begin at least two months in advance with notices sent to the staff directly involved. Don't forget the maintenance staff or food service staff if bag lunches or schedule changes are going to occur. Following the initial notice, ongoing communication with the involved staff is necessary.

SAMPLE INITIAL STAFF COMMUNICATION

> April
>
> The time is fast approaching to begin planning for the annual Field Day events. During this preparation time, we would like to remind you that planning and good communication will insure a successful day for both students and staff.
>
> This year we would like to suggest a change in the type of events conducted on this exciting day. During the past years most Field Days have revolved around a "track meet" format with individual races and relays. In order to involve all students in student-centered cooperative activities in a less competitive environment, I am suggesting the attached activities and format. Students have enjoyed taking part in these activities during physical education classes this year and a Field Day of this type seems a natural extension.
>
> We look forward to these events and working with you to make this another exciting day for our students.

SAMPLE ACTIVITIES AND FORMAT (GRADES 3–5)

Plan for cross-age teams. Each team will consist of representatives from each grade level; e.g., 3 third graders, 4 fourth graders, and 3 fifth graders. Teams will be determined through a random draw of names during the physical education classes three days prior to the event. Each team will participate in four of the five "elective" events and all will participate in the two "required" events. All ten team members must participate in each event entered. Total team points will be recorded by the scorer.

Elective Events:

"Skin the Snake"

1. Team members line up in one line.
2. Reach between your legs with the *left* hand grabbing the *right* hand of the person behind you.
3. On the go signal, the last person in line lies down, the next person backs up (still holding hands), and lies down. This pattern keeps repeating until the entire team is lying down.
4. Once the last person has backed up and lied down, he or she gets back up and goes forward. When all members are back on their feet, the team has finished.
5. SCORING: All teams to successfully complete the activity get 5 points. Teams completing the activity in a time between 20 to 30 seconds get 7 points. Those teams completing the activity in less than 20 seconds receive 9 points.

"Amoeba Race"

1. Five members of each team (3 minimum at one time) form a circle locking arms with their backs to the center of the circle.
2. The remaining five team members are "loose" inside the circle.
3. On the go signal, each team begins to run towards the finish line.
4. SCORING: All teams to finish get 5 points. The first-place team gets 9 points; the second, 8; and so forth.

"Parachute Ball Toss"

1. Team members spread out holding the edge of a parachute.
2. Twenty balls of varying sizes and shapes are placed in the center of the parachute.
3. Each team is given 30 seconds to shake out as many balls as possible.
4. SCORING: One point is awarded for each ball tossed out within the time limit.

"Beachball Balance"

1. Team members pair up in groups of two. Each pair is given an inflated beachball and two wands (plastic baseball bats work just as well).

2. On a 50-yard long field, pairs spread out 10 yards apart.

3. On the go signal, the first pair picks up the wands—each person holding an end of each wand—and balances the beachball on the wands. They run forward, balancing the beachball, to the next pair. They hand off the beachball (without using their hands) to the next pair. This rotation continues until the team has reached the finish line.

4. SCORING: Each team to complete the race gets 2 points. If they complete the race without a drop, they get 5 points. The first team to finish gets 5 additional points, the second team gets 4, and so forth.

"Peanut Race"

1. Each team lines up by a "bucket" of peanuts. Each team member is given a plastic spoon.

2. On the go signal, the first team member picks up a peanut, places it on his or her spoon, and runs a figure-8 course between cones to a finish line 20 yards away.

3. At the finish line the runner places the peanut in an empty bucket, goes back to the starting line, and touches the hand of the next runner who picks up a peanut and begins to run.

4. The relay continues for a predetermined time limit based on the number of peanuts available.

5. SCORING: All teams receive 5 points. Additional points are awarded for each peanut in the finish line bucket at the end of the time limit.

Required Events:

"Water Bucket Relay"

1. This event is similar to "Peanut Race" except each team has a full bucket of water at the starting line and an empty bucket at the end.

2. Each team member has a medium paper/plastic cup that is filled at the start and emptied at the finish.

3. SCORING: All teams receive 5 points. Additional points are awarded for each full cup emptied from the finish line bucket.

"Water Balloon or Egg Toss"

1. Team members are lined up with one person on a starting line and the others approximately two yards apart.

2. On the go signal, the object is passed from the person on the starting line to the next, who passes it to the next, and so forth, until the last person makes the catch.

3. When the last person makes the catch, all of those people take two steps back and begin passing the object back to the starting person who remains stationary.

4. The pattern continues with the "first person" remaining on the starting line and the "last person" moving two steps back upon each successful rotation. The middle people can move as they feel necessary but must stay in one spot while the object is being passed—until the object is dropped and breaks.

5. The team having the greatest distance between the first and last person after all teams are "out" wins.

6. SCORING: All teams get 10 points. The team with the greatest distance receives an additional 10 points.

At the conclusion of all events scores for each team are added. Ribbons or certificates of participation are given to all students, with additional ribbons given to all team members receiving above set criterion; e.g., Level 1 over 100 points; Level 2 between 99–75; Level 3 between 74–50; Level 4 between 49–10. Using this method of awards each participant should be given two ribbons or certificates and feel that they have had a fun and successful day.

SAMPLE ACTIVITIES AND FORMAT (GRADES 6–8)

At the middle-level, students can become more involved in the planning and organization of special events. While keeping to the same philosophy of providing a fun cooperative activity day with limited competition, students—organized by grade or block/homeroom classes—begin planning events three to four weeks prior to the day of the event. Each class has the opportunity to develop one event. They must decide on how it is to be organized, conducted, and scored. The block of students developing the activity is in charge of arranging for all equipment, setting up the event, and monitoring the event during the Field Day. After this process has been completed, a booklet of events is published and distributed to each block of students. During physical education classes or at other prearranged times, students have the opportunity to practice and organize themselves for the events.

Almost-Anything-Goes Day

"Inner Tube Relay"

1. Eight people from each team are involved:

   a. Ball People—2 people running with a ball held between their backs

   b. Inner Tube People—2 people with inner tubes thrown over them

   c. Inner Tube Helpers—4 people to help Inner Tube People

2. A timed event, the course is 2 parallel lines 25 yards apart, with room for four teams to play at one time.

3. At the start two Ball People race to the opposite line with a ball held between their backs. When the Ball People cross the end line, two Inner Tube Helpers throw inner tubes over the waiting Inner Tube People (tubes should reach the persons' waists).

4. The Inner Tube People then move/run to the opposite end line where 2 inner

Tube Helpers lay them on their sides and roll them 10 feet to the final finish line.

5. SCORING: All teams finishing receive 10 points. The team with the best time receives an additional 10 points; second team receives 9 points; third 8; etc.

"Water Balloon Ballet"

1. One person, blindfolded, stands on a ladder. Another person hands him or her water balloons one at a time.

2. Other individual team members carry a box and begin walking across a low balance beam placed in front of the ladder.

3. As the team member walks in front of the ladder, the blindfolded person tries to drop a balloon into the box.

4. After finishing the walk across, the team member gives the blindfolded person a balloon, and hands the box to the next person who begins to walk across.

5. The event continues for 2 minutes.

6. SCORING: All teams receive 10 points. One additional point is added for each balloon in the finished box.

"Frisbee™ Mania"

1. Each team has 5 blindfolded throwers, 5 retrievers, and 1 scorer.

2. The throwing area is made of concentric circles with lines at 10, 20, 30, 40, and 50 feet.

3. To begin, the throwers stand behind the 50-foot line and—on signal—begin to throw. After a throw, the retrievers run to get the Frisbee™ and bring it back to the throwers. The scorer records the circle the Frisbee™ landed in.

4. Each team throws and retrieves for a 4-minute period.

5. SCORING: Points are awarded for each throw according to the circle the Frisbee™ lands in. The 10-foot circle gets 25 points, 20-foot circle gets 20 points, 30-foot circle gets 15 points, and the 40-foot circle gets 10 points.

Summary

Well planned field/play days which complement skills learned in the regular physical education classes not only provide opportunities to participate in a fun activity but also provide students with a chance to utilize a wide variety of skills. The key to success is planning an organization which utilizes a supportive group of assistants and a format which allows all students to be successful.